MW00610840

THE
JOURNEY OF
THE BLOOD

Apostle Halton Horton
Apostle Frank Baio

Published by Purpose Publishing LLC.
1503 Main Street #168 ✻ Grandview, Missouri
www.purposepublishing.com

ISBN: 978-0-6928907-7-6
Copyright ©2017 Frank Baio, Author
Prepared for Publication by Frank Baio Ministries
All Rights Reserved

Printed in the United States of America

This book, or parts thereof, may not be reproduced, stored in a retrieval system, or transmitted in any form or by means – electronic, mechanical, photocopy, recording, or any other – without the prior permission of the publisher.
I have used many sources, and I have always attempted to cite any exact quotations and/or use material that is not under copy-right. Any failure to cite (or locate any unknown source) a quote is simply an oversight on my part.

Unless otherwise indicated, all Scripture quotations are taken from the King James Version of the Holy Bible, copyright ©1982 by Thomas Nelson, Inc. The KJV is public domain in the United States of America. Italics in the text demonstrate the author's emphasis.

Scripture marked NKJV is taken from the New King James Version of the Bible
Scripture marked CJB is taken from the Complete Jewish Bible
Scripture marked NLT   is taken from the New Living Translation of the Bible

Scripture quotations marked AMP are taken from The Amplified® Bible. Old Testament, copyright ©1965, 1987 by Zondervan Corporation. New Testament copyright ©1958, 1987 by the Lochman Foundation. Used by permission.

Scripture quotations marked NIV are from The New International Version®, NIV® of the Holy Bible. Copyright ©1973, 1978 1984, 2011 by Biblica, Inc.™. Used by permissions. All rights reserved worldwide.

Dedication

I want the dedicate this to those who have been influential in my life. I want to thank the Lord Jesus Christ for giving me "the Spirit of Wisdom, Revelation of Jesus Christ and for opening up the eyes and ears of my understanding" and the ability to write this meaningful, important book.

To Apostle Halton (Skip) Horton, thank you so much for the spiritual insight that you have imparted on me over the years.

To Apostle Rufus Troup, for introducing me to Apostle Horton. Thank you also for your ongoing mentoring; that has helped me to mature in God's word and understand biblical leadership and authority more deeply.

To Apostle Verbert C. Anderson, thank you for introducing me to Apostle Rufus Troup and the five-fold ministry of the 7000 More Covenant Fellowship .

And to the many other members of the five-fold ministries in this great fellowship, I want to say thank you for being an example of the believers.

Last but not least, I want to thank my wife, Fran, for standing by my side as a prayer warrior and intercessor. Many are the occasions that we have discussed the Word, and Fran has shared nuggets that the Lord has revealed to her. These nuggets have been inspirational in writing this book.

Apostle Frank Baio, Ph.D.

Foreword

From the Old Covenant to the New Covenant the blood is the foundation of our redemption. In the Old it covered our sins but in the New it removed our sins. The purposes of God are revealed in the New Covenant.

Jesus said this is my blood of the new covenant which is poured out for many for the remission of sins. Matthew 26:28. The blood has done a most marvelous work, which is, that it gives us God. Therefore the blood of Jesus not only atones for our sins that we may not be penalized, but in addition, it restores completely all that was lost in the garden of Eden as well as releases us into newness of life. The blood of Jesus is both for atonement and restoration.

The gospel, the good news is this; the blood of Jesus Christ through the new covenant meets our needs perfectly. There is no necessity to add anything to it, or is there the possibility of subtracting something from it. In redeeming us, he gives us these magnificent blessings in the Lord Jesus Christ who was the perfect sacrifice. "Wow", that is good news.

Apostle Halton Horton

Table of Contents

The Central Theme

In these days of apostasy in the church, we are seeing that many of the core values that we were raised with have been eroded. Core values that are being excluded in many churches: are: true worship, preaching on the death, burial and resurrection of Jesus Christ, speaking on the blood of Jesus, sin and repentance.

The purpose of this book is to give us a clearer understanding of the blood of Jesus Christ. We can see the blood of Jesus as a scarlet thread from Genesis through to Revelation.
THE CENTRAL THEME OF THE BIBLE is the birth, death, burial and resurrection of Jesus Christ. The Bible is the only book that man may read to know God. From Genesis to Malachi the pre – incarnate Jesus Christ describes and predicts what His time on earth will be like. Right down to the finest detail.

These sixty-six books unfold one continuous drama of redemption, paradise lost to paradise regained and creation to the consummation of all things. There is one central theme, the person of Jesus Christ, even by implication in the Old Testament (Luke   24:27). In the Old Testament Christ is anticipated; in the New Testament, he is realized (Matt. 5:17-18). There is one main message: Humankind's problem is sin, and the solution is salvation through Christ (Mark 10:45; Luke 19:10). Such incredible unity is best accounted for by the existence of a divine Mind that the writers of Scripture claimed inspired them. This Mind wove each of their pieces into one mosaic of truth.

Throughout the pages of the Old Testament, we read about Jesus Christ. Even though He is never named in the Old Testament, He appears on every page in the form of symbols, shadows, types, rituals, sacrifices, and prophecies. As we turn to the pages of the New Testament, we encounter Him in the flesh. Here, in the form of a living, breathing human being, is the One who satisfies and fulfills all the symbols and prophecies of Genesis through Malachi. As we move from the Old Testament to the New, we find that one person, Jesus of Nazareth, is the focal point of both Testaments.

See Luke 24:27; Matthew 5:17-18; Mark 10:45; Luke 19:10.

Introduction

The word "blood" occurs 447 times in 357 verses in the Bible. The "Blood" when it refers either directly or symbolically to the blood of Christ is the very heart and core of the Bible, the true foundation of the Christian faith. Any departure from the Biblical message on the "Blood of Christ" is heresy or apostasy. It is clear, that the message of the "Blood of Christ" is of basic importance in the Bible. If you would take the blood out of a human body, death would be the result. If you take the blood out of the Bible, you have a Bible that has no life- giving properties. It is a dead book rather than the "living book" that it claims to be.

See Hebrews 4:12 (AMP) – *"For the word of God is living and active and full of power [making it operative, energizing, and effective]. It is sharper than any two-edged sword, penetrating as far as the division of the soul and spirit [the completeness of a person], and of both joints and marrow [the deepest parts of our nature], exposing and judging the very thoughts and intentions of the heart."*

Over the past several years, The Lord has impressed me with revelation on the blood of Jesus that the enemy has not wanted the church to be aware about. With this knowledge and revelation, we become very dangerous to his Kingdom. The scripture tells us in all your getting, get understanding. Understanding is a twin sister to wisdom. Wisdom is the correct application of knowledge. How many times have you met very educated people? They are so smart, yet cannot get anything done.

My spiritual Father Apostle Halton (Skip) Horton has been encouraging us to begin seeing things as God sees thing. Not in the sense realm, but in the Spirit.

Please keep in mind that there are three applications to all Scripture.

- The First is the Natural or Practical Application

- The Second is the Spiritual Application

- The Third is the Prophetic Application

There is no doubt in my mind that we can read the Scripture today, and get a certain meaning, then come back several weeks later and get another revelation in the very same Scripture.

So, as you study this book on the Blood, ask the Lord to give you the Ephesian 1:17 Prayer: "Lord I pray that you give me the spirit of wisdom, revelation knowledge of Christ and that you open up the eyes and ears of my understanding. Amen."

This book will take you on a journey that will change your life.

Blessings,
Love, Peace and Increase,

Apostle Frank Baio

∾ *1* ∾

The Pre-Incarnate Christ

As we begin this awesome journey of the Bblood, there are several aspects that we will have to consider.

1. As a member of the trinity, The Father, The Son (Jesus) and the Holy Spirit always existed.

2. The understanding that Jesus is and was the Creator.

3. That there is a trail that leads from the book of Genesis through the book of Revelation.

John 1:1-3 (AMP)

1. In the beginning [before all-time] was the Word (Christ), and the Word was with God, and the Word was God Himself.

2. He was [continually existing] in the beginning [co-eternally] with God.

3. All things were made and came into existence through Him; and without Him not even one thing was made that has come into being.

John 10:30 Jesus said, **"I and my Father are one."**

John 1:18 – "No man hath **seen** God at any time, **the** only begotten Son, which is in **the** bosom of **the Father**, he hath declared him."

John 5:37 – "And **the Father** himself, which hath sent me, hath borne witness of me. Ye have neither heard his voice at any time, nor **seen** his shape."

John 6:46 – "Not that any man hath **seen the Father**, save he which is of God, he hath **seen the Father.**"

John 14:9 – "Jesus saith unto him, Have I been so long time with you, and yet hast thou not known me, Philip? he that hath **seen** me hath **seen the Father**; and how sayest thou **then**, Show us **the Father?"**

By stating that Jesus and The Father are one, Jesus was saying that he was the physical embodiment, physical expression and image of the Father.

Five irrefutable facts about Christ

The following scripture gives us insight on how Christ is seen on the old testament.

The first is John 1:1-4,14. In v.1 we read, **"In the beginning was the Word, and the Word was with God, and the Word was God."** It was *later* that **"the Word became flesh (v. 14)."** If the Word was with God before He became flesh, then He obviously existed before His incarnation.

The second is John 6:33-62. There is no need to examine this whole passage. For our purposes, it will suffice just to look at v. 62, where Jesus said to His disciples, **"What if ye shall see the Son of man ascend up where he was before?"**

The third is John 8:58, where Jesus said to the Jews, **"Before Abraham was, I am."** Jesus is obviously stating here that He existed before Abraham.

The fourth is John 17:5, where Jesus was praying to the Father and said, **"And now, O Father, glorify thou me with thine own self with the glory which I had with thee before the world was."** This, too, is an obvious assertion of Christ's preexistence.

The fifth is Phil. 2:6, where Paul, speaking of our Lord, says, **"Who, being in the form of God, thought it not robbery to be equal with God."** This passage is one of the most difficult to interpret, but for our purposes all we need see is that there was a time, before He took on the form of a man, that Christ existed in the form of God. This, too, is an obvious assertion of Christ's preexistence.

Rev. 13:8 – " And all that dwell upon the earth shall worship him, whose names are not written in the book of life of the Lamb slain from the foundation of the world. To be slain before the foundation of the world, means to have existed before the world was made."

The subject of the pre-incarnate existence of Christ **(Christophany)**, and His pre-incarnate works, is an important subject which is frequently neglected in the teaching ministry of the local church. It is important for four reasons.

First, His preexistence is a necessary attribute. If Christ did not exist prior to His incarnation, then He cannot be God.

Second, it is important that the Christian have a firm knowledge of the pre-incarnate Christ in order to avoid being tossed by the winds of false doctrine which Satan is constantly blowing our way through the vehicle of the false cults.

Third, it gives the Christian a greater appreciation of the unity of the Scriptures.

And fourth, it gives the Christian a greater understanding of certain passages of the Bible.

Christ's Pre-Incarnate Existence

What is the significance of a scarlet thread?

The Bible mentions a scarlet thread in several different contexts, from an unusual childbirth to the high priestly garments to the conquest of Canaan.

One reference to the scarlet thread in the Bible occurs during the birth of the twin sons of Judah and Tamar (Gen. 38:27–30). As Tamar was giving birth, the arm of one twin, Zerah, reached out of the birth canal, and immediately the midwife tied a scarlet thread to the baby's wrist to designate Zerah as the firstborn. As it turned out, however, Zerah was not the firstborn; the arm was withdrawn into the womb, and the other twin, Perez, was born first.

In the case of Perez and Zerah, the scarlet thread was to indicate who was to have the designation and privileges of the firstborn. To all appearances, Zerah seemed to be the one, but God had different plans, and Perez was the firstborn. In God's providence, it was through Perez that the line of the Lord Jesus Christ proceeded (Matt. 1:3).

The Bible also mentions scarlet thread or scarlet yarn as part of the tabernacle's curtains (Exo. 26:1) and the high priest's ephod (Exo. 28:6), along with threads of gold, blue, and purple. Scripture does not comment on the significance of those colors in the curtains or ephod, but some commentators surmise that the gold, blue, and purple foreshadow Christ's glory, heavenly origin, and kingly position, while the scarlet thread represents Christ's atoning work on the cross through the shedding of His blood.

Another significant mention of scarlet thread is in Joshua 2. Two spies had been sent to Jericho in advance of the Israelites' taking of that city. The spies were hidden in Jericho by Rahab the harlot, who expressed her faith in Israel's God and protected the spies (see Heb. 11:31). Rahab allowed the Hebrew spies to escape from Jericho by letting them down through her window by means of a rope made of scarlet thread. As they departed, the spies told Rahab, "Tie this cord of scarlet thread in the window" (Josh. 2:18), with the promise that she and her household would be kept safe in the coming invasion. By faith, Rahab obeyed: "And she tied the scarlet cord in the window" (Josh. 2:21).

Later, when the walls of Jericho fell down and the Israelites took the city, Joshua commanded that Rahab and her family be spared (Josh. 6:22–23). Marking her home was, of course, the "cord of scarlet thread." It's easy to dismiss the color of Rahab's rope as mere coincidence, but the scarlet color is significant. The rope in her window was a sign of her faith and led to her salvation, as she was not destroyed with the rest of Jericho. The scarlet rope—the color of blood—worked for Rahab much as the blood of the Passover lamb had worked during the exodus: every home marked with blood was spared death that night (Exo. 12:13). God's mercy and forgiveness of Rahab the harlot was signified by a rope of scarlet thread, which becomes a symbol of the blood of Christ.

Theologians and Bible students sometimes refer to "the scarlet thread running through the Bible." By this they mean that the Bible's theme is Jesus Christ and His sacrifice for the redemption of mankind. The blood of Christ runs throughout the entire Bible, symbolically. It is seen in the animals killed in Eden to provide garments for Adam and Eve, the ram that took Isaac's place on the altar of Moriah, the Passover lamb, the institution of the sacrificial system, the scarlet rope of Rahab, and the thousands of years of sacrifices performed at the tabernacle and temple. The scarlet thread runs all the way up to John the Baptist's declaration, "Look, the Lamb of God, who takes away the sin of the world!" (John 1:29) and to the foot of the cross, where Jesus finally says, "It is finished." (John 19:30).

"Without the shedding of blood there is no forgiveness." (Heb. 9:22), and that's why the symbolism of the scarlet thread in the Bible is significant. The scarlet thread is the theme of atonement found throughout the pages of Scripture.

As stated above, it is essential that the preexistence of Christ be proven in order to prove His deity. In this section, the fact of Christ's pre-incarnate existence will be established.

Old Testament Evidence

Theophanies (God) and Christophany (Christ) – The pre-incarnate Christ

Old Testament Christophanies. A Christophany is an appearance of God in a physical form. These Old Testament Christophanies were none other than Christ Himself. If He appeared before His incarnation, then He obviously existed before His incarnation.

The Old Testament records a number of Christophanies. A Christophany is a pre-Bethlehem appearance of Christ. Most Bible theologians hold that the recurring angel of the Lord episode in the Old Testament is to be identified with Christ himself. This theological position is strongly suggested by the following two key passages.

The first is found in Genesis 48:16 where the dying patriarch, Jacob, is blessing his two grandchildren. The old founder of Israel prays:

"The angel who redeemed me from all evil, bless these lads…" (Gen. 48:16).

As no regular angel can redeem men, it is assumed the angel here is actually Christ.

The second passage is found in Judges 13 where a barren couple has just learned from the angel of the Lord about the future birth of Samson. In gratitude, Manoah (the father), requests the name of the angel that he might call the babe after him. Note the answer, however:

"And the angel of the Lord said unto him, Why asketh thou thus after my name, seeing it is secret?" (Jdg. 13:18).

This word, "secret," is from the same Hebrew root word found in Isaiah 9:6, where it is translated "wonderful."

"For unto us a child is born, unto us a son is given: and the government shall be upon his shoulder: and his name shall be called Wonderful, Counsellor, The mighty God, The everlasting Father, The Prince of Peace" (Isa. 9:6).

Inasmuch as we know the "wonderful" in this verse refers to Christ, it is highly probable that Judges 13:18 does as well.

Let us now examine some of these Old Testament theophanies.

A. He appeared to Hagar, Abraham's Egyptian wife (Gen. 16:7-14). The first biblical reference to the angel of the Lord occurs here as he tenderly ministers to a pagan and pregnant Egyptian girl.

B. He appeared to Abraham (Gen. 18:1; 22:11-13). These two appearances came at critical times in Abraham's life. One (Gen. 18) concerned itself with the destruction of Sodom, and the other (Gen. 22) with the last-minute salvation of Isaac.

C. He appeared to Jacob (Gen. 28:13; 32:24-32; 48:16). It will be remembered that Christ not only appeared to Jacob, but also wrestled with him. (See Gen. 32.). This was doubtless that same divine One he had seen standing atop a ladder some twenty years before. (See Gen. 28.).

D. He appeared to Moses (Ex. 3:2; 23:20; 33:18-23). These three occasions were all connected with Mt. Sinai.

The <u>first</u> occasion was *near* the mountain.

"And when the Lord saw that he turned aside to see, God called unto him out of the midst of the bush, and said, Moses, Moses. And he said, Here am I. And he said, Draw not near here: put off thy shoes from off thy feet, for the place whereon thou standest is holy ground" (Ex. 3:4, 5).

The <u>second</u> was on *the* mountain.

"Behold, I send an angel before thee, to keep thee in the way, and to bring thee into the place which I have prepared" (Ex. 23:20).

The <u>final</u> occasion was *in* the mountain.

"And it shall come to pass, while my glory passeth by, that I will put thee in a clift of the rock, and will cover thee with my hand while I pass by" (Ex. 33:22).

    E. He appeared to Joshua (Josh. 5:13-15). He appears to Joshua on the eve of the battle against Jericho and introduces himself as the captain of the Lord's host.

    F. He appeared to Gideon (Jdg. 6:11-24). The angel of the Lord finds a very discouraged Gideon threshing wheat beside a wine press to hide it from the oppressing Midianites.

    G. He appeared to Samson's parents (Jdg. 13).

    H. He appeared to Isaiah (Isa. 6:1-13). Isaiah is allowed to see more of the glory of the pre-incarnate Christ than any other Old Testament prophet.

    I. He appeared to three young Hebrews in the fiery furnace (Dan. 3:25). How thrilling are the astonished words of pagan king Nebuchadnezzar which accompanied this appearance:

"Then Nebuchadnezzar the king was astonished, and rose up in haste, and spake, and said unto his counselors, did not we cast three men bound into the midst of the fire? They answered and said unto the king, True, O king. He answered and said, Lo, I see four men loose, walking in the midst of the fire, and they have no hurt; and the form of the fourth is like the Son of God" (Dan. 3:24, 23).

    J. He appeared to Daniel (Dan. 6:22; 7:9-14). The first of these appearances was in a lion's den.

"Then said Daniel unto the king, O king, live forever. My God hath sent his angel, and hath shut the lion's mouth, that they have not hurt me..." (Dan. 6:21, 22).

The second appearance was in a vision.

"I beheld till the thrones were cast down, and the Ancient of days did sit, whose garment was white as snow, and the hair of his head like the pure wool: his throne was like the fiery flame, and his wheels as burning fire. A fiery stream issued and came forth from before him: thousands and thousands ministered unto him, and ten thousand times ten thousand stood before him: the judgment was set, and the books were opened. I beheld then because of the voice of the great words which the horn spake: I beheld even tfill the beast was slain, and his body destroyed, and given to the burning flame. As concerning the rest of the beasts, they had their dominion taken away: yet their lives were prolonged for a season and time. I saw in the night visions, and, behold, one like the Son of man came with the clouds of heaven, and came to the Ancient of days, and they brought him near before him. And there was given him dominion, and glory, and a kingdom, that all people, nations, and languages, should serve him: his dominion is an everlasting dominion, which shall not pass away, and his kingdom that which shall not be destroyed" (Dan. 7:9-14).

K. He appeared to Zechariah (Zech. 1:8-13; 2:8-11; 3:10; 6:12-15). In this book, Zechariah describes Christ as protecting Jerusalem (1:8-13), measuring Jerusalem (2:8-11), cleansing Jerusalem (3:10), and building Jerusalem (6:12-15).

New Testament Evidence

The New Testament abounds with evidence for Christ's preexistence. Some of the evidence is implied, but other evidence is directly asserted. Also, His pre-incarnate works imply preexistence. It would be unnecessary to cite every bit of evidence here, but hopefully enough will be cited to be convincing.

The Scarlet Thread

Implications from His Work

We shall see that Christ's works include:,

- creation.

- the preservation of the universe.

- the sustaining of the children of Israel in the wilderness.

In order for Christ to have done these things, which happened prior to His incarnation, He had to have existed. Therefore, Jesus Christ existed from "the beginning" along with God the Father.

The Journey of the Scarlet Thread

Leviticus 17:11-14

Leviticus 17:11 "For the life of the flesh is in the blood: ...."

Leviticus 17:14 "For it is the life of all flesh; the blood of it is for the life thereof: therefore, I said unto the children of Israel, Ye shall eat the blood of no manner of flesh: for the life of all flesh is the blood thereof: whosoever eateth it shall be cut off."

 – Blood is mentioned over 400 timesx in the Bible.

 – Eternal life is in the blood of Jesus

There's a scarlet thread throughout the entire Bible. ..

It could be said that the entire Bible has a "scarlet thread" of redemption weaved through it. This "blood-red" thread begins in Genesis, in the Garden of Eden, with God Himself shedding the blood of animals to clothe Adam and Eve in their sin. This thread is the "bloodline" of the Bible. By following this bloodline, we can discover the greatest story ever told, the story of our Redeemer, Jesus Christ, and the story of salvation for all mankind through salvation in His blood. The scarlet thread continues all the way into the book of Revelation where, through the apostle John's eyes, we see a great multitude from every tribe, tongue and nation standing before God, those "who have washed their robes and made them white in the blood of the Lamb.". When you find the "bloodline" in the Bible, you find the redemptive heart of God — for the world, and for you.

God started weaving the scarlet thread in Eden when He clothed Adam and Eve in animals (the first blood sacrifice). He hooked in the thread when He prophesied about the "seed of the woman" who would crush the head of the serpent. This thread is seen again in the life of Abel, who offered a sacrifice acceptable to God — one of the blood of animals. The bloodline shows up again in Noah's burnt offering after the flood — a "soothing aroma" to God.

The scarlet thread can be seen again in God's covenant with Abraham, a covenant which required blood sacrifice. It is revealed again in the substitution of the ram for Isaac, - who was laid on the altar by His Father Abraham in obedience to God. On the night of the Exodus, this mysterious "bloodline" was unveiled even more in the Passover. The Angel of Death "passed over" every house that had applied the blood of the lamb to the frame of their doorway. In the middle of God's wrath, all in those houses were safe "under the blood"."

Is it not amazing, when God's wrath caused the walls of Jericho to fall flat, that Rahab's house - built into the wall - was safe? One rope of scarlet thread made the difference. All n her house were safe, and all their belongings were safe. The scarlet thread tied in the window had the same effect in her house as the blood of the lamb on the doorposts during Passover night.

The continuing scarlet thread of redemption is even illustrated in the sea that Israel crossed in the Exodus – it was the RED Sea.

As God took Israel from the wilderness into the Promised Land, the scarlet thread of Scripture became a literal river of atoning blood. Every day, at the entrance of the Tabernacle, countless sins were spoken over the heads of countless innocent animals who poured out their blood in sacrifices prophetic of the coming "Lamb of God" who would take away the sins of the world. This daily prophetic bloodbath continued for centuries. It was still in process in the temple of Jerusalem right up to the night in which Jesus the Lamb of God was arrested – on Passover night itself!

Rahab-Jericho was conquered by a miracle of God. Israel was told to march around the city in silence for seven days. On the seventh day, they were told to march around it seven times, then to shout a great shout. When they shouted, the city wall collapsed. The army of Israel went in to destroy the city. Rahab and all her relatives were saved, however, and taken in as part of God's people. Even her belongings were saved. All because of her obedience to tie the scarlet thread in her window!

That "scarlet thread" in her window not only saved her from destruction, but also brought her into a whole new life. She became a mother in the royal bloodline of Israel! Rahab - prostitute and heathen - became the mother of Boaz, who married Ruth. She ended up the great grandmother of King David, and in the direct lineage of Jesus (see Ruth chapter 4 and Matthew chapter 1). What a grand epic of God's redeeming power!

That night, the Passover was fulfilled. The long anticipated sacrificial blood of the True Lamb began to flow.

The blood of Jesus first spilled in the garden of Gethsemane. Under the agony of the burden coming on His soul, Jesus' sweat became as drops of blood. Within hours, He was in the cruel hands of Roman soldiers, with blood streaming down

His back. Thirty - nine lashes from cords laced with metal and glass tore His back to shreds. Blood flowed from His head as the "crown" of two-inch thorns was pressed into His skull. As He hung in agony on the cross, more blood poured out through His pierced hands and feet. Blood flowed internally as well, as He was beaten and "bruised for our iniquities." After hours of agony, He cried "It is finished!", and then He died. Blood (and water) again flowed, out from His side as a soldier drove a sword into Him.

By the time of His resurrection three days later, the scarlet thread had become an unbreakable and unchangeable new covenant, - put in effect by God Himself. This was the covenant of blessing that was first promised to Abraham, now sealed in Christ's blood. That blood was holy, sacrificial, redemptive, divine, and life- giving. That blood assures eternal and complete salvation for all who believe. The mystery of the scarlet thread had now been unveiled as the Father's plan of eternal and complete redemption through the blood of Christ!

John 1:29".... Behold the Lamb of God, which taketh away the sin of the world."

1 John 1:7".... the blood of Jesus Christ his Son cleanseth us from all sin."

Examples of the Scarlet Thread

1. **Adam & Eve: Blood covered their shame. Gen. 3:21 –** "-Unto Adam also and to his wife did the Lord God make coats of skins, and clothed them."

2. **Abel: Blood was the accepted offering. Gen. 4:4 —** "And Abel, he also brought of the firstlings of his flock and of the fat thereof. And the Lord had respect unto Abel and to his offering.":

3. **Abraham & Isaac: Ram substituted for a son. Gen. 22:13 –** "And Abraham lifted up his eyes, and looked, and

behold behind him a ram caught in a thicket by his horns: and Abraham went and took the ram, and offered him up for a burnt offering in the stead of his son."

4. **Passover: Blood of a lamb. Ex. 12:13** – "- And the blood shall be to you for a token upon the houses where ye are: and when I see the blood, I will pass over you, and the plague shall not be upon you to destroy you, when I smite the land of Egypt."

5. **Temple sacrifice: The blood of animals. Lev. 16:21** – " - And Aaron shall lay both his hands upon the head of the live goat, and confess over him all the iniquities of the children of Israel, and all their transgressions in all their sins, putting them upon the head of the goat, and shall send him away by the hand of a fit man into the wilderness.":

6. **The Scarlet thread in Ps 22:1** – "- My God, My God why hast thou forsaken me."
Ps 22:6-8 – "- ... despised of people .... Laugh me to scorn... Let him deliver
. The scarlet thread leads to: THE CROSS!"

7. **The Scarlet thread in the Prophets. – Is 53:5** – "He was wounded for our transgressions ... With his stripes, we are healed."
Daniel 9:24--26 – "24. Seventy weeks are determined upon thy people and upon thy holy city, to finish the transgression, and to make an end of sins, and to make reconciliation for iniquity, and to bring in everlasting righteousness, and to seal up the vision and prophecy, and to anoint the most Holy.

25. Know therefore and understand, that from the going forth of the commandment to restore and to build Jerusalem unto the Messiah the Prince shall be seven weeks, and threescore and two weeks: the street shall be built again, and the wall, even in troublous times.

26. And after threescore and two weeks shall Messiah be cut off, but not for himself: and the people of the prince that shall come shall destroy the city and the sanctuary; and the end thereof shall be with a flood, and unto the end of the war desolations are determined."

8. **The Scarlet thread in the Gospels. Jn. 1:29.**
   John said, "Behold (Look), the Lamb of God, who takes away the sin of the world." Jn. 1:29
   Matthew 26:27–28 – "- 27 And he took the cup, and gave thanks, and gave it to them, saying, Drink ye all of it;

28 For this is my blood of the new testament, which is shed for many for the remission of sins."

9. **The Scarlet thread in the Epistles**

A. **Redeems Us from A Wasted Life**
   1 Peter 1:18–19 – "- 18 Forasmuch as ye know that ye were not redeemed with corruptible things, as silver and gold, from your vain conversation received by tradition from your fathers; 19 But with the precious blood of Christ, as of a lamb without blemish and without spot."

B. **Washes Away the Stain Of Our Sin**
   1 John 1:7 – " - But if we walk in the light, as he is in the light, we have fellowship one with another, and the blood of Jesus Christ his Son cleanseth us from all sin."

C. **Brings Us into A Relationship With God**
   Ephesians 2:13 – "But now in Christ Jesus ye who sometimes were far off are made nigh by the blood of Christ."

✎ 3 ✎

The Blood from Genesis to The Revelation

Throughout scripture we can see the trail of the blood. The first example is the sacrificing of the animals in the garden of Eden to cover Adam and Eve's sins. One of the last references is in the book of Revelation "They overcame him by the word of their testimony and by the Blood of the Lamb (Rev. 12:11).

A major reference to the blood is that, "The life of the flesh is in the blood, and I have given it to you upon the altar to make atonement for your souls; for it is the blood that makes atonement for the soul" (Lev. 17:11).

Just as "the life of the flesh is in the blood," so the life of Christianity is in the atoning, life- giving blood of the Lord Jesus Christ. Jesus said, "I am ... the life" (John 14:6). He is the life of God, made living in the believer. Paul said, "Christ lives in me" (Gal. 2:20). Christ lives in every born again believer because the believer, by faith, is a partaker of the life- giving blood of Jesus. We are children of God by the blood. Therefore, we are "blood relatives" of God through the living blood of Jesus the Son of God, who is God the Son.

If the atoning blood of Jesus is rejected, and the rejecter continues willfully to reject eternal life through the blood, after knowing the truth that "the blood of Jesus Christ His Son cleanses us from all sin" (1 John 1:7), for that person "there no longer remains a sacrifice for sins" (Heb. 10:26-28). Christ atoned for our sins in His own body on the tree.

The First Shedding of Blood (Genesis. 3:21)
A Reminder of the Atonement – Atonement means to cover.
To cover
"The Lord God (Jesus) made clothes of skin, and clothed them"."
(Gen. 3:21). When the first man and woman sinned, God did not
drive them from the garden robed in their man made, bloodless
religion. The Word says, "Then the eyes of both were opened,
and they knew that they were naked; and they sewed fig leaves
together and made themselves coverings" (Gen. 3: 7). Adam
and Eve experienced a new feeling; for the first time they felt
guilt, which caused them to fear God and to hide.

God judged the man and woman, and before He drove them
from the garden, He (Jesus) sacrificed animals; the innocent
shed their blood for the guilty. What an excellent illustration
of the Lord Jesus "who Himself bore our sins in His own body
on the tree" (1 Pe. 2:24). Peter also tells us that we have been
redeemed "with the precious blood of Christ, as of a lamb
without blemish and without spot" (1 Peter 1:18, 19).

Adam and Eve must have watched as Jesus selected the animals;
and so they witnessed the first shedding of innocent blood,
knowing that it was because Adam had failed God (1 Cor. 15:45
49). As they watched, they learned that God in His sovereign
grace provided a covering, a propitiation for their sins. Not
a cover up, but a cover—a promise of payment in full to blot
out sin and to make atonement for mankind (Lev. 17:11). They
departed from the garden knowing that "without shedding of
blood there is no remission"—no forgiveness of sin (Hebrews
9:22).

So, the blood of Jesus Christ covers the sins of the believer and
robes him in the righteousness of Christ (Romans 10:1- 4).

Abel's Blood Offering (Genesis 4:3- 7)
A Reminder That He was to be the sacrificial Offering
Why did God reject Cain's offering and accept Abel's? A careful
examination of the two brothers and their offerings will answer

this question, and will give you a fresh glimpse of "the Lamb of God who takes away the sin of the world" (John 1:29).

Cain's offering was not an act of saving faith. Cain believed that God existed, and had come to worship Him. But he had the wrong offering, the wrong attitude, and the wrong motive (Matt. 7:21- 23). Cain did not do the will of God; he acted according to his own will. He had "a form of godliness but denying its power" (2 Timothy 3:5).

Abel's offering, on the other hand, was an act of saving faith (Eph. 2:8, 9). "By faith Abel offered to God a more excellent sacrifice than Cain, through which he obtained witness [from God] that he was righteous" (Heb. 11:4). By faith Abel offered a lamb for the remission of sins, and God declared him righteous.

Cain's offering was bloodless; it may have been equal in cost to Abel's, but it was without the shedding of blood (Heb. 9:22).

Abel's offering was a blood sacrifice; it was a type of the Lamb of God who shed His blood to redeem lost souls (1 Pet. 1:18, 19).

Cain's offering was a type of salvation by works (Titus 3:5)

Abel's offering was a type of salvation by grace (Eph. 1:7).

Cain's offering was a type of dead religion.

Abel's offering was a type of life: "The life of the flesh is in the blood [the life of Christianity is in the blood of Christ], and I have given it to you upon the altar to make atonement for your soul; for it is the blood that makes atonement for the soul" (Lev. 17:11).

Cain's bloodless offering was rejected by God.

Abel's blood offering was accepted by God, and Abel was made righteous with the righteousness of Jesus who would atone for his sins (2 Cor.inthians 5:21).

The Offering of Isaac (Genesis 22:1- 19)
A Reminder that He was the substitute, the provision
This chapter is awesome in many ways and is a treasure of spiritual wealth, and awesome in many ways. We can never reach its height or depth, nor exhaust its spiritual significance. Gradually we see beneath the surface, and slowly begin to discern the purpose of God in this unique picture of Jesus Christ, our substitute. When Abraham and Isaac left the land of Moriah, after seeing God provide a ram to take the place of Isaac, they knew that "the eternal God is your refuge, and underneath are the everlasting arms" (Deut. 33:27). How can anyone read of this amazing event and not stand in awe of Jehovah Jireh?. "And Abraham called the name of the place, **The Lord Himself is The Provision**" (Gen. 22: 14). And God did provide a ram **(Jesus)** to take the place of Isaac, because Abraham believed God and obeyed Him without asking, "Why, Lord?"

Genesis 22:1 tells us that "God tested Abraham." God did not tempt him toward evil in the sense of luring him to fall, because "God cannot be tempted by evil, nor does He Himself tempt anyone" (James 1:13). Rather, He tested Abraham to show the quality of this man who was His friend. God puts Abraham's faith to the supreme test. In Genesis 22:2, he said to Abraham, "Take now your son, your only son Isaac, whom you love (*"For God so loved the world that He gave His only begotten son. That whosoever beliveth in Him Shall not perish but, have everlasting Life" – John 3:16*), and go to the land of Moriah, and offer him there as a burnt offering on one of the mountains of which I shall tell you"

The mountain in the land of Moriah, where Abraham built the altar to sacrifice Isaac, is a mountain range. Several important biblical sites are located in this range. It is believed to be the plateau on which Solomon built the temple. Some believe that the Most Holy Place stood over the exact spot where Abraham built his altar. But, more importantly, this is where Golgotha is located. On Mount Moriah we see that God provided a ram that was caught in the thicket (Thorn Bushes). These thorn bushes have a name' they are called the Jerusalem thorns. These are the thorns that were formed into a crown and then place on the head of Jesus.

The Passover Blood (Exodus 12:1- 36)
A Reminder of the Cross
Exodus chapter 12 is one of the great chapters of the Bible. It displays deliverance from slavery for Israel, and judgment of Pharaoh and all Egypt. The Lord said to Moses, "I will bring one more plague on Pharaoh and on Egypt" (Exodus 11:1). The "one more plague" was death for the firstborn, wherever there was no Passover blood on the doorpost and the lintel.

Exodus 12:13 – "And **the blood** shall be to you for a token upon **the** houses where ye are: and **when** I **(Myself, The Pre-Incarnate Christ) see the blood, I** will **(Myself, The Pre-Incarnate Christ)** pass over you, and the plague shall not be upon you to destroy you, **when I** smite **the** land of Egypt."

When the Lord (Jesus, the Pre-Incarnate Christ) passed through the land of Egypt, He began by going through the land of Goshen (where the Jews lived). Jesus would later state that "the rain falls on the just and the unjust alike (Matt. 5:45)." As the Lord made his way through the land of Goshen, He saw the blood on the door post. This was a reminder of His sacrificial work on the cross. Accompanying The Lord was the Angel of Death to enforce the Father's instruction. That was to kill the first born in all the houses of Egypt, beginning with the house of Pharaoh.

The Passover Lamb

1. The Passover lamb is a type of the Lord Jesus Christ who redeems not with silver or gold, but with His own life-giving blood (1 Pet. 1:18, 19). Paul reminds the Corinthian church that Christ is our Passover Lamb who was sacrificed for us (1 Cor. 5:7).

a. The Passover lamb "shall be without blemish, a male of the first year" (Exo. 12: 5). The Passover lamb is a type of Jesus, "who knew no sin." (2 Cor. 5:21) He was without blemish (2 Cor. 5:21), and even challenged His enemies to find sin in Him: "Which of you convicts me of sin?" (John 8:46).

b. The Passover lamb was to be separated from the sheep or goats, from the tenth to the fourteenth day. This separation period was a time of examination, to make certain that the Passover lamb was without blemish. The Passover lamb is a type of Jesus, "who is holy, harmless, undefiled, separate from sinners, and has become higher than the heavens" (Heb. 7:25- 28).

c. The Passover lamb was to be killed: "And you shall take a bunch of hyssop, dip it in the blood that is in the basin, and strike the lintel [the crossbeam] and the two doorposts with the blood that is in the basin" (Exo. 12: 22). The blood of the Passover lamb is a type of the blood of Jesus, who hung upon the cross and shed His precious blood for the remission of our sins (John 19:28- -37). The blood on the crossbeam and on the two doorposts is a picture of the blood stained cross.

2. God said to Israel, "The blood shall be a sign for you on the houses where you are. And when I see the blood, I will pass over you" (Exo. 12:13). Now God did not say, when I see your good works, or your moral character, or your self-righteousness, or your religion, or the laws you keep, I will pass over you. No! He said, "When I see the blood, I will pass over you" (Exo. 12: 13). Remember, without the blood of Jesus there is no forgiveness of sin (Heb. 9:22).

The Day of Atonement in the Old Testament (Lev. 16:1- 34)
A Reminder that He was our Scapegoat
God gave us a scapegoat: – His son on the cross.

He became sin for the world: – His blood was the cost.

The 16th chapter of Leviticus is rich in typology, with Christ as the fulfillment of each type. He is our atonement for all of our sins. The biblical meaning of the word atone is to cover, to expiate, and to pay the penalty for sins. To reconcile, or to achieve "at one-ment" with God, is a part of the atoning death of Christ. To atone is to bring the sinner from a state of enmity with God to a place of union or oneness with Him (2 Cor. 5:18).

The Day of Atonement was to be repeated on the tenth day of the seventh month, year after year. It was a day of rest; the Israelites were to do no work. It was a day of repentance. God said, "You shall afflict your souls" (Lev. 16: 29). On the Day of Atonement, the high priest entered the Most Holy Place and sprinkled the atoning blood upon the mercy seat, to atone for all the sins of the congregation, including those sins committed unintentionally or in ignorance (Lev. 4:1- 35).

Compare the high priest with the Lord Jesus Christ:

1. He is a type of Christ in his office as a mediator. He was the "go between"; he alone stood between God and man. ONCE each year he was to go alone before God with atoning blood, while the congregation waited to be reconciled to God (Lev. 16: 16, 34). Christ fulfilled this office of the high priest as recorded in Hebrews: "He is the Mediator of the new covenant, by means of death" (Heb. 9:12 15). "For there is one God and one Mediator between God and men, the Man Christ Jesus" (1 Tim. 2:5).

2. The high priest offered the blood of a bull to make atonement for his own sins (Lev. 16: 6). In this offering he is not a type of Christ; the Lord Jesus Christ did not have to make atonement for His own sins, because He is the sinless One (Heb. 7:27, 28). The Scriptures say that He "committed no sin" (1 Pet. 2:22), that "in Him there is no sin" (1 John 3:5), and that He "knew no sin" (2 Cor. 5:21).

3. Two goats were presented before the Lord at the door of the tabernacle. Aaron was to cast lots for them; one would be sacrificed and the other would be the "scapegoat" (Lev. 16: 7, 8).

   a. The atoning blood of the sacrificial goat, which was sprinkled on the mercy seat to cover the sins of the people (Lev. 16: 7- 9), is a type of Christ, our High Priest, who "entered the Most Holy Place once for all, having obtained eternal redemption" (Heb. 9:11- 14).

   b. The scapegoat is also a type of Christ. Aaron, after atoning for the sins of the people with the blood of the sacrificed goat, was to take the live goat and lay his hands on its head, confessing all the iniquities and sins of Israel. Then he was to send it into the wilderness (Lev. 16: 21, 22), so that those sins might be lost and out of sight forever. Christ bore our sin in His own body on the cross, was placed in the tomb, and rose on the third day. Christ alone will wear the scars of His sacrifice in His holy body. In His resurrection, He fulfills the type of the living scapegoat (Matt. 28:1-¬7).

   The term Scapeg Goat comes from the Hebrew definition of Azazel, the meaning is "goat of departure." Lev. 16:8 should then read: "one lot for the Lord and the other for the goat of departure." Because the first goat called "a lot for the Lord," the translators wanted the Hebrew word Azazel, to be a representation of someone. Therefore, some translators have concluded that Azazel must represent an evil spirit or Satan.

What is Azazel?.

—According to Talmudical interpretation, the term "Azazel" designated a rugged mountain or precipice in the wilderness from which the goat was thrown down. Another etymology connects the word to "Uza" and "Azael," **the fallen angel**, to whom a reference is believed to be found in Gen. vi. 2, 4. In accordance with this etymology, the sacrifice of the goat atones for the sin of fornication of which those angels were guilty (Gen. l.c.).

The Miracle of the "Lot"

The first of these miracles concerns a random choosing of the "lot" which was cast on the Day of Atonement (Yom Kippur). The lot chosen determined which of two goats would be "for the Lord" and which goat would be the "Azazel" or "scapegoat." During the two hundred years before 30 CE, when the High Priest picked one of two stones, again this selection was governed by chance, and each year the priest would select a black stone as often as a white stone. But for forty years in a row, beginning in 30 CE, the High Priest always picked the black stone! The odds against this happening are astronomical. In other words, the chances of this occurring are 1 in approximately 5,479,548,800 or about 5.5 billion to one!

The lot for Azazel, the black stone, contrary to all the laws of chance, came up 40 times in a row from 30 to 70 AD! This was considered a dire event and signified something had fundamentally changed in this Yom Kippur ritual. This casting of lots is also accompanied by yet another miracle which is described next.

The Miracle of the Red Strip

The second miracle concerns the crimson strip or cloth tied to the Azazel goat. A portion of this red cloth was also removed from the goat and tied to the Temple door. Each year the red cloth on the Temple door turned white as if to signify the atonement of another Yom Kippur was acceptable to the Lord. This annual event happened until 30 CE when the cloth then remained crimson each year to the time of the Temple's destruction. This undoubtedly caused much stir and consternation among the Jews. This traditional practice is linked to Israel confessing its sins and ceremonially placing this nation's sin upon the Azazel goat. The sin was then removed by this goat's death. Sin was represented by the red color of the cloth (the color of blood). But the cloth remained crimson; that is, Israel's sins were not being pardoned and "made white."

As God told Israel through Isaiah the prophet:

"Come, let us reason together, saith the Lord: though your sins be as scarlet [crimson], they shall be white as snow; though they be red like crimson, they shall be as [white] wool" (Isaiah 1:18).

The clear indication is that the whole community had lost the Lord's attention in relation to something that occurred in 30 CE. The yearly atonement achieved through the typical Yom Kippur observance was not being realized as expected. Atonement apparently was to be gained in some other way. Who or what would provide the atonement for another year?

Though not mentioned in the Scriptures and long before 30 C.E. during the 40 years Simon the Righteous was High Priest, a crimson thread which was associated with his person always turned white when Simon entered the Temple's innermost Holy of Holies. The people noticed this. Also, they noted that "the lot of the Lord" (the white lot) came up for 40 straight years during Simon's priesthood. They noticed that the "lot" picked by the priests following Simon would sometimes be black, and sometimes white. Also, they noticed that , the crimson thread would sometimes turn white, and sometimes not. The Jews came to believe that if the crimson thread turned white, that God approved of the Day of Atonement rituals and that Israel could be assured that God forgave their sins. But after 30 CE, the crimson thread never turned white again for 40 years unt, the destruction of the Temple and the cessation of all Temple rituals!

What did the Jewish nation do in 30 CE to merit such a change at Yom Kippur? By some accounts, on April 5, 30 CE (i.e., on the 14th of Nisan, the day of the Passover sacrifice) the Messiah,

Yeshua, was cut off from Israel and put to death as a sacrifice for sin. Through this event, there is a transference of the atonement that was no longer achieved through the two goats as offered at Yom Kippur. Like an innocent Passover lamb, the Messiah was put to death even though no fault was found in Him! But unlike Temple sacrifices or the Yom Kippur events (as detailed above) where sin is only covered over for a time, the Messianic sacrifice comes with the promise of forgiveness of sins through grace given by God to those who accept a personal relationship with Messiah. This is essentially a onetime event for each person's lifetime and not a continual series of annual observances and animal sacrifices. The mechanism providing forgiveness of sin changed in 30 CE.

When we take an objective look at the events of 30 CE, who can doubt that it was indeed the true year of the crucifixion and resurrection of the true Messiah that God sent to Israel? Who can deny that He is the one and only true Messiah? Who else has fulfilled all the prophecies of the Old Testament — including the amazing prophecy of Daniel 9 and the "70 weeks," coming at the very year predicted for the Messiah to appear?

The scarlet thread was a symbolical reference to Isaiah. 1: 18; and the Talmud tells us that during the forty years that Simon the Just was high priest, the thread actually turned white as soon as the goat was thrown over the precipice: a sign that the sins of the people were forgiven. In later times the change to white was not invariable: a proof of the people's moral and spiritual deterioration, that was gradually on the increase, until forty years before the destruction of the Second Temple, when the change of color was no longer observed.

The Day of Atonement revealed in the New Testament (John 20:17)

1. Volitional. (The meaning of volitional is: will: an act of making a choice or decision; also: a choice or decision made) Jesus Christ willingly chose to be God's sacrificial

Lamb to take away the sins of the world (John 1:29). None of the Old Testament sacrifices could bring eternal redemption. The high priest had to repeat the sacrifice and enter the Most Holy Place once every year to atone for the sins of the people (Lev.iticus 16:12- 16). All the animal sacrifices were imperfect types of Jesus Christ, our perfect blood sacrifice (Heb.rews 9:11- 14).

2. Motivated by love. The love of the Holy Trinity (Father, Son, and Holy Spirit) for us is manifested in the vicarious death of Jesus Christ (John 3:16).

3. An act of rational obedience (Phil. 2:5- 8). In God's eternal economy, He was "the Lamb slain from the foundation of the world" (Rev. 13:8). Therefore, He knew beforehand every agonizing moment that He would endure on the cross, and the ignominious shame He would experience (Heb. 12:2).

4. The end of all animal sacrifices. "For if we [Hebrew believers in Christ] sin willfully after we have received the knowledge of the truth [that Christ died for our sins, was buried and rose from the dead], there no longer remains a sacrifice for sins" (Heb. 10:26- 29). "For Christ is the end of the [ceremonial] law for righteousness to everyone who believes" (Rom.ans 10:4).

It was necessary for Christ, our High Priest, to enter the Most Holy Place in heaven after His resurrection and sprinkle His own blood upon the mercy seat to make atonement for the sins of Old and New Testament believers (Heb. 9:11, 12).

Without the Shedding of Blood (Hebrews 9:22)

"Without the shedding of blood there is no remission" (Heb. 9:22).

This is one of God's imperatives. Without the atoning blood of the Lord Jesus, there is no remission of past, present, or future sins. Without His blood, there is no remission of sins of action or neglect, nor is there remission of sins committed in ignorance nor is there remission for the sin of doing the right thing in the wrong way. Unless the sinner is cleansed from sin by the blood of God the Son, there is no remission at all. Without shedding of blood there is:

1. No justification. To be justified is to be declared judicially righteous because you have been washed and made white in the blood of the Lamb (Rom. 3:24- 26; cf. Rev. 1:5).

2. No redemption. To redeem is to buy back. God's only begotten Son shed His blood to redeem (buy back) sinful man (Eph. 1:7).

3. No forgiveness. "In whom we have redemption through His blood, the forgiveness of sins" (Col. 1:14).

4. No cleansing. The blood of Jesus continues to cleanse us from sin day after day (1 John 1:7).

5. No atonement. "For it is the blood that makes atonement for the soul" (Lev. 17:11).

6. No sanctification. To sanctify means to set apart for God's use. The blood of Jesus sets every cleansed believer apart for salvation and service (Heb. 13:12).

7. No victory. The saints (all true believers) will overcome Satan, sin, and all the powers of darkness by the blood of Jesus Christ the Lamb (Rev. 12:11). No wonder Peter calls it "the precious blood of Christ" (1 Pet. 1:18, 19).

$\backsim 4 \sim$

The Garden of Gethsemane?

The garden at Gethsemane, a place whose name literally means "oil press," is located on a slope of the Mount of Olives just across the Kidron Valley from Jerusalem. A garden of ancient olive trees stands there to this day. Jesus frequently went to Gethsemane with His disciples to pray (John 18:2). The most famous events at Gethsemane occurred on the night before His crucifixion when Jesus was betrayed. Each of the Gospel writers describes the events of that night with slight variations, so reading the four accounts (Matt. 26:36-56, Mark 14:32-52, Luke 22:40-53 and John 18:1-11) will give an accurate picture of that momentous night in its entirety.

As the evening began, after Jesus and His disciples had celebrated the Passover, they came to the garden. At some point, Jesus took three of them—Peter, James and John— to a place separated from the rest. Here Jesus asked them to watch with Him and pray, so they would not fall into temptation (Matt. 26:41), but they fell asleep. Twice, Jesus had to wake them and remind them to pray so that they would not fall into temptation. This was especially poignant because Peter did indeed fall into temptation later that very night when three times he denied even knowing Jesus. Jesus moved a little way from the three men to pray, having charged His disciples with their duty to pray for themselves. Jesus walked to a different area — about a stone's throw away, Luke tells us — and began to pray Himself. Our Lord's prayer, while it took up a fair amount of time, could be summed up in these words, "Father, if you are willing, take this cup from me; yet not my will, but yours be done" (Luke 22:42).

For what is our Lord praying? Let us examine this point. According the book of Revelation, we see that Jesus was slain from the foundation of the earth (see Rev. 13:8 – "And all that dwell upon the earth shall worship him, whose names are not written in the book of life of the Lamb slain from the foundation of the world"). Therefore, what was Jesus praying to the father? The only conclusion we can come to is that the only event that Jesus had never experienced was being separated from the Father. Sin separates man from God.

Yet, Jesus submitted to the Father's will. He was "exceedingly sorrowful unto death," but God sent an angel from heaven to strengthen Him (Luke 22:43).

The events that occurred in the Garden of Gethsemane have reverberated down through the centuries. The passion Jesus displayed on that extraordinary night has been told again and again. Even our language has been affected by these events, giving us such phrases as "he who lives by the sword dies by the sword" (Matt. 26:52); "the spirit is willing, but the flesh is weak" (Mark 14:38); and "sweating drops of blood" (Luke 22:44). Of course, the most important impact of this night was the willingness of our Savior to die on the cross in our place in order to pay the penalty for our sins. God "made Him who knew no sin, to be sin for us, that we might become the righteousness of God in Him" (2 Cor. 5:21). This is the gospel of Jesus Christ.

Matthew Matt. 26:36-44
36 Then Jesus went with them to a place called Gethsemane, and He told His disciples, sit down here while I go over yonder and pray.
37 And taking with Him Peter and the two sons of Zebedee, He began to show grief and distress of mind and was deeply depressed.
38 Then He said to them, my soul is very sad and deeply grieved, so that I am almost dying of sorrow. Stay here and keep awake and keep watch with Me.
39 And going a little farther, He threw Himself upon the ground on His face and prayed saying, My Father, if it is possible, let this cup pass away from Me; nevertheless, not what I will [not what I desire], but as You will and desire.

40 And He came to the disciples and found them sleeping, and He said to Peter, What! Are you so utterly unable to stay awake and keep watch with Me for one hour?

41 All of you must keep awake (give strict attention, be cautious and active) and watch and pray, that you may not come into temptation. The spirit indeed is willing, but the flesh is weak.

42 Again a second time He went away and prayed, My Father, if this cannot pass by unless I drink it, your will be done.

43 And again He came and found them sleeping, for their eyes were weighed down with sleep.

44 So, leaving them again, He went away and prayed for the third time, using the same words.

Luke 22:43-44 (NKJV)

43 Then an angel appeared to Him from heaven, strengthening Him.

44 And being in agony, He prayed more earnestly. Then His sweat became like great drops of blood falling down to the ground.

This bleeding was a result of the intense agonizing prayer.

Perspiration fell from Jesus' face like great drops of blood as He wrestled with the pain of taking upon Himself the sin of the world and **in turn enduring separation from His Father.**

The night before Jesus Christ was crucified, He prayed in the Garden of Gethsemane. It is in Luke's Gospel where we see that His sweat was like drops of blood: "And being in agony, He prayed more earnestly. Then His sweat became like great drops of blood falling down to the ground" (Luke 22:44). Hematidrosis is a rare, but very real, medical condition where one's sweat will contain blood. The sweat glands are surrounded by tiny blood vessels. These vessels can constrict and then dilate to the point of rupture where the blood will then effuse into the sweat glands. Its cause: —*extreme anguish*. In the other Gospel accounts, we see Jesus' level of anguish: "My soul is overwhelmed with sorrow to the point of death" (Matt. 26:38; cf. Mark 14:34).

The intense anguish and sorrow Jesus felt was certainly understandable. Being God, Christ knew "all that was going to happen to Him" (John 18:4). He knew in painstaking detail the events that were to follow soon after He was betrayed by one of His very own disciples. He knew He was about to undergo several trials where all of the witnesses against Him would lie. He knew that many who had hailed Him as the Messiah only days earlier would now be screaming for His crucifixion (Luke 23:23). He knew He would be flogged nearly to the point of death before they pounded the metal spikes into His flesh. He knew the prophetic words of Isaiah spoken seven centuries earlier that He would be beaten so badly that He would be "disfigured beyond that of any man" and "beyond human likeness" (Isa. 52:14). Certainly, these things factored into His great anguish and sorrow, causing Him to sweat drops of blood. Yet, there was more.

Medical doctors confirm that at times of intense fear or agony, a person's blood vessels can literally break beneath the skin and blood will begin to come out of their pores like sweat.

Out of Jesus' pores came sweat and blood because of the anxiety, the fear, and the turmoil He was experiencing.

But in this place of turmoil, the obedient nature of Christ led Him and us as a result to a place of victory over our will. Jesus declared with eternal consequence, "not My will but your will be done".(Matt. 26:39)"

Jesus was showing us what intercessory was all about: . wWhen you place yourself in the place of a person in need. It is where you agonize to such an extent that you feel the hurt of what that person is going through.

The first place Jesus shed His blood was in a garden because the first place we lost the power of God's blessing was in another garden, the Garden of Eden. It was in the garden that man chose to rebel against God and exercise the right of his will to live in his mind independently from God.

Philippians 2:5 — **"Let this mind** be in you which was also in Christ Jesus"

1 Corinthians 2:16 – -For "who has known **the mind of the** Lord that he may instruct Him?" But we have **the mind of Christ.**

Luke 22: 45 – " When He rose up from prayer, and had come to His disciples, He found them sleeping from sorrow."

Matt. 26:45-49

45 Then He returned to the disciples and said to them, are you still sleeping and taking your rest? Behold, the hour is at hand, and the Son of Man is betrayed into the hands of especially wicked sinners [whose way or nature it is to act in opposition to God].

46 Get up, let us be going! See, my betrayer is at hand!

47 As He was still speaking, Judas, one of the twelve [apostles], came up, and with him a great crowd with swords and clubs, from the chief priests and elders of the people.

48 Now the betrayer had given them a sign, saying, The One I shall kiss is the Man; seize Him.

49 And he came up to Jesus at once and said, Hail (greetings, good health to You, long life to You), Master! And he embraced Him and kissed Him with [pretended] warmth and devotion.

John 18:4-6

4 Jesus therefore, knowing all things that would come upon Him, went forward and said to them, "Whom are you seeking?"

5 They answered Him, "Jesus of Nazareth. Jesus said to them, "I am He." And Judas, who betrayed Him, also stood with them.

6 Now when He said to them, "I am He," they drew back and fell to the ground.

Matthew 26:50-56

50 Jesus said to him, Friend, for what are you here? Then they came up and laid hands on Jesus and arrested Him.

51 And behold, one of those who were with Jesus reached out his hand and drew his sword and, striking the body servant of the high priest, cut off his ear.

52 Then Jesus said to him, put your sword back into its place, for all who draw the sword will die by the sword.

53 Do you suppose that I cannot appeal to My Father, and He will immediately provide Me with more than twelve legions [[q]more than 80,000 72,000] of angels?

54 But how then would the Scriptures be fulfilled, that it must come about this way?

55 At that moment Jesus said to the crowds, have you come out with swords and clubs as [you would] against a robber to capture Me? Day after day I was [r]accustomed to sit in the [s]porches and courts of the temple teaching, and you did not arrest Me.

56 But all this has taken place in order that the Scriptures of the prophets might be fulfilled. Then all the disciples deserted Him and, fleeing, escaped.

In the garden Jesus was betrayed was approached by Judas Iscariot. The betrayal of Jesus was sealed with a kiss from Judas. As the soldiers and religious leaders came to arrest Jesus, Peter pulled out a sword in order to defend Jesus. Peter then cut off the ear of one of the temple guards, Malchus, (John 18:10), and as only Jesus could do, Jesus picked up the fallen ear. I can just see the next step: Jesus picked up the ear from the dirty floor. Then shook off the dirt and dust, and then miraculously re-attach the ear on the head of the soldier. Can you imagine how Malchus must have felt? No doubt his life would never be the same.

The Convergence of Two Dimensions
Jesus of Two Dimensions
- ### The natural
- ### The spiritual

Jesus then addressed Peter and said "Peter, put your sword away! He that lives by the sword will die by the sword. Don't you realize that I can call (12) legions of angels to defend me?" A legion is 6,000 soldiers. Jesus was saying that He could summon 72,000 angels!? The prophet Isaiah states in the book of Isaiah 37:36: – **"Then the angel of the LORD went forth, and smote in the camp of the Assyrians a hundred and fourscore and five**

thousand: and when they arose early in the morning, behold, they were all dead corpses." Based on the words of Jesus, these 72,000 could conceivably kill over 13,320,000,000, nine billion more than the world population. Source -The Dake's Bible Commentary

Jesus had to explain His statement to Peter; , the reason was that at that moment, Peter was not saved. **See 1 Cor. 2:14** – "But **the natural man** receiveth not **the** things of **the** Spirit of God: for **they** are foolishness unto him: neither can he know **them,** because **they** are spiritually discerned." Peter had yet not been spiritually born. Jesus had not completed His assignment. When Jesus would complete His assignment, a new creation would be born — The Church.

Jesus was not limited by the natural realm. Jesus had set the stage for all of the spiritual activities surrounding the cross and the events that were about to develop.

After this, Judas arrived, followed by a large number of men with swords, lanterns, and clubs—a Roman cohort (of 300-600 men) as well as officers from the chief priests and Pharisees. Judas called to Him — calling Him "Rabbi," or teacher — and kissed Him, a traditional greeting at the time. In case they didn't get the picture, Jesus asked the soldiers who they were looking for. When they said "Jesus the Nazarene," Jesus responded, "I am He." Whereupon the guard and soldiers drew back and fell to the ground.

Why did the soldiers fall back when Jesus said, "I am He"? Bible versions add the "He" for clarification, but what Jesus actually said was "I AM." This is the name of God (Exodus 3:14). Jesus revealed Himself as God. Faced with the name — the power and identity — the guards fell in fear of His glory.

Nevertheless, they arrested Him and took Him to Pontius Pilate, while the disciples scattered in fear for their lives.

$\backsim$ *5* $\sim$

Who Was Present at the Crucifixion?

At one time or another, most of us have seen Hollywood's portrayal of the crucifixion of Christ. The most recent being Mel Gibson's hit movie, "The Passion of Christ".

As we continue the journey of the blood, we need a new perspective on the most important event in history. All accounts are from a natural, historic perspective. We need to look at the cross from a spiritual view. When we do this, our eyes will truly be opened.

Let me pray: Father, as we explore the events surrounding the death of you son Jesus, our Lord and Savior, please, remove the scales from our eyes. "Let us see beyond what we see." I pray that you give us the spirit of wisdom, revelation knowledge of

Christ and that you open the eyes and ears of our understanding. We come against every work of the enemy that would hinder these readers from seeing these events from your view. I declare and decree the blood of Jesus be on the reader. Amen!

Jesus was tried in court before Pilot and found innocent, and falsely sentenced, due to the pressure of the religious leaders of that day. We are aware that Jesus suffered a humiliating torture reducing Jesus to resemble raw meat. Tortured to such a degree that he became un-recognizable. Stripped naked, crowned with a crown of thorns that were 2"-3" long. These thorns were filled with a neurotoxin in them. (A neurotoxin is: a poisonous substance that acts on the nervous system and disrupts the normal function of nerve cells)

When Jesus finally arrived at Golgotha (The Place of the Skull), He was nailed to a wooden cross. Then they hoisted Him up in the air so that all of the people present would see the power of the Roman Empire against anyone that would dare to challenge their authority.

Who Was at the Crucifixion?

In the Natural and Historical view, at the foot of the cross we have the following:

- The women, the soldiers, the centurion, the chief priests, members of the Sanhedrin,

- The group of His own disciples standing far away the vast multitudes of people from the whole surrounding country.

- The multitudes gathered at the cross included all sorts and conditions of men, representative crowds. The whole scene being a picture and a prophecy of how, through all the centuries, every sort and condition would be gathered to the uplifted Cross of the Son of man.

Let's peel off the scales from our eyes and see in that other dimension

On each side of the cross that Jesus was nailed, were two malefactors (Thieves). These were truly guilty for their offences.

The two thieves represent two sides:

1. The Penitent – Righteous

2. The Un-repentant- un-righteous

These two thieves: one righteousness and one un-righteousness

Of these two thieves, we see that each sees Jesus in a different light. On one side, there is a mocking thief and on the other there is a penitent thief.

The mocking thief says, "if you are the Christ get of the cross and us with you."

Whereas the penitent thief said, "Remember me when you get into your kingdom."

Jesus' response to the penitent thief was, "This day you will be with me in paradise." (For further information about Paradise, see the chapter: "What happened during the three days?").

THE BATTLE OF THE AGES

The foot of the cross is what the battle is all about. It is important for us to realize that the reason that you and I have been under constant attack is explained in John 10:10 – "The enemy comes forth to steal, kill and destroy, But, (Jesus) I have come to give life and life more abundantly."

From the days of the Garden of Eden, Satan has desired all that God gave to mankind:. Authority, Power, Ruler-ship, Dominion, Power, Fellowship and Relationship. At the crucifixion, mankind thought that all was lost, but, the resurrection was only three days away.

As we peel away the layers of the natural and step into the spiritual realm, we will see who really was at the crucifixion.

Just close your eyes, and ask the Lord to give you spiritual insight.

On One Side Of The Cross - All of Heaven Lined up on the sideline of this panoramic view

On one side of the cross, we see that God the Father was present. Jesus spoke to Him. Jesus, said "Daddy why have you forsaken me?" (or Why have You turned your back on Me?)

We know that with the Father being present so was The Holy spirit (both being co-equal with God and both being omnipresent).

With the Father and the Holy Spirit, cherubim and Seraphim were also present as they are the protectors and defenders of the throne of God.

God also has a messenger angel named Gabriel and a general of His army named Michael the Archangel. With Michael, the archangels were at least the 12 legions of angels (72,000 angels). These angels were at Jesus' disposal in the Garden of Gethsemane. These twelve legions of warring angels had the ability to destroy mankind (12) times over. See the list below of all that we present on God's side. "If God is for us who can stand against us."(Rom. 8:31)

On the Opposing Side- All of Satan's forces Lined up on the sideline of this panoramic view

On the opposing side Lucifer, (the archenemy of Christ). Was leading all of these evil spirits. According to the Gospel of John "All things were created by the Word (Jesus) (Col. 1:16)" Therefore, Lucifer hated and despised His creator. The cross became the means for the destruction of The Creator. Seeing Jesus go through all of the demeaning and degrading process of crucifixion caused Lucifer to celebrate. Jesus, his longtime enemy was in his hands and soon would be destroyed once and for all.

Lucifer also has a chain of command. The Apostle Paul tells us that "we wrestle not with flesh and blood but against principalities, against powers, against Rulers of the darkness of this world, the strongman and against spiritual wickedness in high place." (Eph. 6:12).

As The time of Jesus' ultimate death approached, all of Lucifer's hoard were celebrating (partying) that their boss' arch enemy would eventually succumb to death. The celebration became more intense as Jesus was weakening. With the intensification of the celebration, the humans witnessing this awful crucifixion became a wild mob, calling out Barabbas as their champion and not Jesus, their the savior and deliverer. During the crucifixion, Jesus had taken on the sins of mankind. These satanic spirits knew that Jesus would be in their ugly hands in the place of the unrighteous dead (See the chapter "what happened during those three days"). With this realization, came the revelation that they would have to keep Him in the place of torment by force. Lucifer knew the scripture that David the Psalmist declared referring to the Messiah: "That he should still live forever, and not see corruption" (Ps. 49:9). The word corruption means decomposition or decay. Therefore, these evil spirits knew that they were going to have to restrain Jesus until his body was to decompose.

THESE ARE THE THREE WITNESSES TO THE DEATH OF JESUS

THE CROSS IS THE GREAT DIVIDE

The Heavenlies

The Penitent Thief
God the Father
The Holy Spirit
Seraphim
Cherubim
Zoe Spirits
Angel of Death
Thrones
Dominions
Virtues
Powers
Principalities
Archangels
Angels
Ministering Spirits

Humanity at the Foot of the cross

In the Natural and Historical view, we notice:
The women,
The soldiers,
The malefactors,
The centurion,
The roman soldiers
The chief priests,
The false accusers
The Sanhedrin,
His own disciples standing far away

Satan's Kingdom

The Un-Repentant Thief
Principalities
Powers,
Rulers of darkness
Spiritual wickedness in high places
Demons.
Spirit hatred
Spirit of Anger
Lying Spirit
Perverse Spirit
Spirit of Bondage
Spirit of Fear
Seducing Spirit
Spirit of Anti-Christ
Spirit of Death

There were three different reactions at the cross:

On one side we see Satan and his minions were celebrating. Their celebration was based on a miscalculation that by killing Christ they would be rid of Him forever. The principalities and powers of darkness were assembled around the cross, casting the hellish shadow of unbelief into the hearts of men. The powers of darkness did not understand God's master plan, that Jesus had to come to redeem man from the curse of sin and all associated with sin. They certainly did not understand the resurrecting Power of God. Can you imagine the taunting and celebrating that must have been going on as Jesus was hanging in humiliation, suffering, through pain and agony between heaven and earth? They had not read the script.

Those that were followers of Jesus, in His earthly ministries, were in deep in-consolable sorrow. Mary, the mother of Jesus, had a broken heart. Many of them had their hopes and dreams crushed. You see, they were looking at Jesus as their deliverer and not their Savior. These mourners knew that Jesus said, "I am the resurrection and the life." However, these mourners too were miscalculating. They were operating in the natural and not in the spirit. The Roman centurion, truly had a better understanding of the events that they had all witnessed, when he stated, "Truly this was the Son of God."(Matt. 24:54)

On the other side we have God and the heavenly host. These events unfolding right before them was extremely sobering. The Father knew the master plan. There must have been an overpowering desire to destroy mankind. Yet, it was the love for humanity that Jesus demonstrated on the cross that prevented this destruction. This Love of Christ was beyond comprehension. This stayed the hand of God.

With grief and amazement, Heaven viewed Christ hanging upon the cross, blood flowing from His wounded temples and sweat tinged with blood standing upon His brow. From His hands and feet, the blood fell, drop by drop, upon the rock drilled for the foot of the cross. The wounds made by the nails gaped as the weight of His body dragged upon His hands. His labored breath grew quick and deep, as His soul panted under the burden of the sins of the world. All of heaven was filled with wonder when the prayer of Christ was offered in the midst of His terrible suffering, --"Father, forgive them; for they know not what they do" (Luke 23:34). Yet, there stood men, formed in the image of God, joining to crush out the life of His only begotten Son. What a sight for the heavenly universe!

Just picture this scene: Jesus is un-recognizable in the cross, having been reduced to something resembling raw meat. Then to make matters worse, Jesus takes the sins of world upon Himself. At which time the Father must turn His back on His own son. God is so Holy that He cannot look upon Sin. If The father were to have continued to look upon Jesus, the Father would have had to kill His own son.

I am reminded of the Garden of Gethsemane. When Jesus told Peter to put his sword away,"I have at my disposal twelve legions of angels."(Matt 26:53)

As the Father turned His back on His son, I can see in the spirit, Michael the Archangel and all of the angels with their hands on their swords, say to God, "God, just say the word and we will destroy mankind. You created them before and you can recreate them again."

Just then, I hear Jesus say "Father, forgive them for they know not what they do." (Luke 23:34)

These six hours were the darkest in history. As Jesus gave up His spirit, historians tell us that there was a total solar eclipse, lightening flashed and the thunder roared and the earth quaked. The Lord showed me that this was all of creation convulsing because it creator has been slain. The Scripture states: "The earth is the Lord and the fulness thereof"(Psalm 24:1)

Simply put, the meaning of the cross is death. The success of the cross is that it's victim dies. From about the 6th century BC until the 4th century AD, the cross was an instrument of execution that resulted in death by the most torturous and painful ways. In crucifixion, a person was either tied or nailed to a wooden cross and left to hang until dead. Death would be slow and excruciatingly painful; in fact, the word *excruciating* literally means "out of crucifying." However, because of Christ and His death on the cross, the meaning of the cross today is completely different.

In Christianity, the cross is the intersection of God's love and His justice. Jesus Christ is the Lamb of God who takes away the sin of the world (John 1:29). The reference to Jesus as the Lamb of God points back to the institution of the Jewish Passover in Exodus 12. The Israelites were commanded to sacrifice an unblemished lamb and smear the blood of that lamb on the doorposts of their homes. The blood would be the sign for the Angel of Death to "pass over" that house, leaving those covered by blood in safety. When Jesus came to John to be baptized, John recognized Him and cried, "Behold, the Lamb of God, who takes away the sin of the world!" (John 1:29), thereby identifying Him and God's plan for Him to be sacrificed for sin.

One might ask why Jesus had to die in the first place. This is the over-arching message of the Bible — the story of redemption. God created the heavens and the earth, and He created man and woman in His image and placed them in the Garden of Eden to be His stewards on the earth. However, due to the temptations of Satan (the serpent), Adam and Eve sinned and fell from God's grace. Furthermore, they have passed the curse of sin on to their children so that everyone inherits their sin and guilt. God the Father sent his one and only Son into the world to take on human flesh and to be the Savior of His people. Born of a virgin, Jesus avoided the curse of the fall that infects all other human beings. As the sinless Son of God, He could provide the unblemished sacrifice that God requires. God's justice demanded judgment and punishment for sin; God's love moved Him to send His one and only Son to be the <u>propitiation</u> for sin.

Because of Jesus' atoning sacrifice on the cross, those who place their faith and trust in Him alone for salvation are guaranteed eternal life (<u>John 3:16</u>). However, Jesus called His followers to take up their cross and follow Him (<u>Matt. 16:24</u>). This concept of "cross-bearing" today has lost much of its original meaning. Typically, we use "cross-bearing" to denote an inconvenient or bothersome circumstance (e.g., "my troubled teen is my cross to bear"). However, we must keep in mind that Jesus is calling His disciples to engage in radical self-denial. The cross meant only one thing to a 1st-century person — death. "Whoever would save his life will lose it, but whoever loses his life for my sake will find it" (<u>Matt. 16:25</u>). Galatians reiterates this theme of death of the sinful self and rising to walk in new life through Christ: "I have been crucified with Christ. It is no longer I who live, but Christ who lives in me. And the life I now live in the flesh I live by faith in the Son of God, who loved me and gave himself for me" (<u>Gal. 2:20</u>).

There are places in the world where Christians are being persecuted, even to the point of death, for their faith. They know what it means to carry their cross and follow Jesus in a very real way. For those of us who are not being persecuted in such fashion, our job is still to remain faithful to Christ. Even if we are never called to give the ultimate sacrifice, we must be willing to do so out of love for the One who saved us and gave His life for us.

<u>Remember This:</u>
Calvary expresses the love of God.
The resurrection explains the power of God.

~ 6 ~

THE 7 PLACES JESUS SHED HIS BLOOD

Beloved, even as we celebrate the Passover Feast and Resurrection weekend, allow me to draw your attention to the significance of Jesus' death on the cross and the shedding of His blood. It is important for us to know what the Lord has done for us and to walk in His victory. As you may already know, God declares in His Word that blood shall be the only means of atonement. *Heb. 9:22 "And almost all things are by the law purged with **blood**, and without **shedding of blood** is no remission."* It is the blood of Jesus that bought our freedom for us.

The number seven means completion. Isa. 53: 3-5 "He was despised and rejected of men; a man of sorrows, and acquainted with grief: and we hid as it were our faces from Him: He was despised, and we esteemed Him not there is no beauty that we should desire Him. Surely, He hath borne our grief (sicknesses) and carried our sorrows (diseases): He was wounded for our transgressions, He was bruised for our iniquities and the chastisement for our peace was upon Him and by His stripes we are healed."

On the cross, when He said, "it is finished" at that moment He atoned for our sins, transgressions, iniquities, sicknesses, diseases, peace and salvation. He said I have completed the work that I came to do. He paid the price so that you would not have to be sick, broke, busted and disgusted.

You may also know that 7 is the number of God. If you like, you can call it His signature because about every one of His works, you will find this number represented. For example, when giving Aaron instructions for the atonement on the mercy seat, God said the blood was to be sprinkled there 7 times. *"And he shall take of the bullock, and sprinkle it with his finger upon the mercy seat eastward; and before the mercy seat shall he sprinkle of the blood with finger seven times." (Leviticus 16:17).*

Now, take note that God also had Jesus shed His blood at 7 places, each instance with its own significance. I will therefore now take you through the process of His death on the cross for us and the *7 losses* His blood repurchased for us. When you understand what the blood of Jesus did for you, you will never again stay in bondage in any area of your life. No. You will demand your freedom! For now, this, as Jesus has already won the victory, yet we find God's people still oppressed. Why is this? Because Jesus took the victory for us but the devil is still squatting on the property. It is upon us to serve him with the eviction notice. This is ENFORCING THE VICTORY OF CHRIST. Make no mistake, Satan is no gentleman; he will not go voluntarily just because Jesus defeated him on the cross, no, HE MUST BE FORCED OUT!

Jesus did all He could do to free you and me. The rest is up to us. If we go after the enemy, he will have to give up and let go of what belongs to us, but if we do not demand it, then the situation will remain just as if Jesus never came in the first place. Which is why you need to hear this and act.

Now see this verse: *Isa 53:5 "But He was wounded for our transgressions; He was bruised for our iniquities; the chastisement of our peace was on Him; and with His stripes we ourselves are healed."* You can see right their different reasons for the sufferings of the Master. From the wounds, bruises, chastisements and stripes. There is more, just read on.

SO HERE IS THE LIST OF THEM:

1. Jesus shed blood at the Garden of Gethsemane.
Verse where it happened: Luke 22:44 "And being in anguish,

he prayed more earnestly, and his sweat was like drops of blood falling to the ground."
Jesus shed His blood in the garden when He sweat great drops blood.

- This is That He is ever making intercession on our behalf

What was redeemed there: Our Willpower.
Garden of Gethsemane - Jesus won back our Will Power

Jesus shed His blood in the Garden of Gethsemane to redeem my will

Matthew 26:19 1Peter 1:18-19

- Matt. 26:39- " Oh My Father, if it is possible, let this cup pass from Me; nevertheless, not as I will, but as You will."

- Luke 22:43-46- "Then an angel appeared to Him from heaven, strengthening Him. And being in agony, He prayed more earnestly. Then His sweat became like great drops of blood falling to the ground. "Reflection Song: "Gethsemane" sung by Melanie Hoffman

In the Garden of Eden, Eve was accosted by the serpent, Satan, and she was duped into eating of the forbidden fruit. Then Adam came along, and know right now that he was not duped into eating of the fruit, he made a conscious choice to partake of it, a decision to go against God, and when he did so, that brought sin into the world and gave Satan a place in this world. Jesus then sweat blood in the garden of Gethsemane and in doing so, He undid what Adam had done in the Garden of Eden. How? Adam opened the door to sin coming into the world that day in the Garden of Eden, and Jesus on another day in a garden, in fear of what He was about to face, so much fear that He was sweating great drops of blood, gave us a way out from the sin in the world. He did so right at that very moment because just as Adam made a conscious decision to partake of the fruit and bring sin in, Jesus was making a conscious decision to be the sacrifice to remove that sin. He set us free right at that very moment in that garden, when despite great fear He spoke saying, "Father, if thou be willing, remove this cup from me: nevertheless, not my will, but thine, be done". Unlike Adam who made a decision to go against the will of God, choosing his own will instead, Jesus; even in such tremendous fear and agony stated, your will be done Father. Right then and there in that garden, Jesus undid what Adam had done so long ago in another garden. Those great drops of blood shed in that garden can cleanse us and bring us into the will of our Father. Pray those great drops of the blood of Jesus over your spouses "will", purging them of self-willfulness and self-righteousness and bringing them into the will and the ways of the Lord for their lives and your marriage.

It was in the Garden of Eden that Adam lost his willpower (i.e. ability to say no to sin and to all that is evil and of the flesh) and it is in in another Garden (Gethsemane) that Jesus gained this power back for us i.e. when He said no to following His own desires. When Jesus went to the Garden of Gethsemane, He knew full well what He was going to redeem for us there: our willpower. So, when he was tested, He finally prayed: *"Father, if thou be willing, remove this cup from me: nevertheless, not my will, but thine, be done".*

In the Garden of Gethsemane (place of pressing): He knew the suffering that He would have to go through on the cross and He cried out to God the Father and said: "If it be thy will let this cup pass from me." He was in such agony that He sweat drops of blood. There he gave you back your will power. He paid the price for you to be able to say, "I will quit drinking, I will quit smoking, I will not throw temper fits, I will not watch pornography, and I will not commit adultery."

Now, through Christ we have power to say no to sin, every kind of bondage and selfish self-seeking that we may get into.

2. He shed blood at the whipping post.

Verse where it happened: Mat 27:26 "Then he released Barabbas to them. And when he had scourged Jesus, he delivered Him to be crucified."

Jesus shed His blood when he was being scourged with the cat of nine (9) tails applied to his back.

- "By His stripes, we were healed"

- Paul said, "cast all your cares on Him for He cares for you"

He took 39 stripes on His back that you might be healed. There healing was provided for every disease: cancer, muscular dystrophy, diabetes, aids, warts, any known or unknown sickness.

What was redeemed there: Jesus won back Our "Health."

Jesus shed His blood at the whipping post. He took 39 stripes upon His back.
Stripes/Wounds on His Back – Jesus won back our "Health"

- 1 Peter 2:24 – Who Himself bore our sins in His own body on the tree, that we, having died to sins, might live for righteousness – by whose stripes you were healed.

- Matt. 8:17 – That it might be fulfilled, which was spoken by Isaiah the prophet: "He Himself took our infirmities and bore our sicknesses." Reflection Song: "By His Wounds"

Jesus was whipped to break the curse of sickness and disease from my life.

Isaiah 53:5 I Peter 2:24

John 19:1 Then Pilate therefore took Jesus, and scourged him.
Isa 53:5 But he was wounded for our transgressions, he was bruised for our iniquities: the chastisement of our peace was upon him; and with his stripes we are healed.
1Pe 2:24 Who his own self bares our sins in his own body on the

tree, that we, being dead to sins, should live unto righteousness: by whose stripes ye were healed.

Jesus bled from the whipping He endured at the whipping post, the scourging, by which we are healed. We have all been taught this teaching often, by His stripes we are healed physically. So, we know to pray the blood of the stripes over our bodies health issues.

It is well known that there are 39 root-diseases in the world. Jesus while being whipped at the post was given 39 lashes. Each one of those beatings was for the sake of every sickness man would ever suffer for. Let me draw your attention to the truth that that every sickness is a curse for breaking the law of God. It is the blood of Jesus that breaks this curse for us. There is now no disease that Jesus cannot heal. His body was broken up so that ours can be made whole. However, these sicknesses may also come due to negligence and later be enforced by the kingdom of darkness.

Jesus also symbolized this breaking of His body in the breaking of the bread at the Last Supper; He was showing how His body would be broken for our healing. Therefore, everyone who receives Him qualifies to receive His healing power. The curse of sickness is broken by His blood!

Isaiah 53:5 KJV "But he was wounded for our transgressions, he was bruised for our iniquities: the chastisement of our peace was upon him; and with his stripes we are healed."

The scourge was the cruelest form of punishment as one was whipped 39 times using a whip known then as a 'cat of nine tails'. This whip had nine strands each with pieces of sharp bones and metal and a heavy piece of lead at the end of the cord. According to the law, one could be whipped 40 times but many times they would stop one short of it at 39. This was because 40 whips were often found fatal. However, the whip left one totally broken. Psalms 129:3 says, "The plowers plowed upon my back..." and Isaiah 50:6 says, "I gave my back to the smiters; and my cheeks to them that plucked off the hair." Jesus went through untold suffering so that we may be healed.

Jesus shed blood through His face when they pulled out His beard.

- "He Is Touched by The Feelings of Our Infirmities"

3. **He shed blood internally - from the intense beating.**
   Verse where it happened: Mat 27:26 "Then he released Barabbas to them. And when he had scourged Jesus, he delivered Him to be crucified."

   What was redeemed: Our forgiveness and liberty from the hold of transgressions and iniquities.

   Jesus Bled Inside (Bruised) - Jesus won Deliverance from "Inner Hurts and Iniquities"

   Jesus bled on the inside when he was bruised to break every iniquity, to expel the inner drive of sin from my life. Isaiah 53:5; 2 Corinthians 2: 21 2 Corinthians 5;17

- Isaiah 53:5 - "But He was wounded for our transgressions, He was bruised for our iniquities; the chastisement for our peace was upon Him, and by His stripes we are healed.

But it says that Jesus was bruised for our iniquities also. Wounded for our transgressions. Not only did Jesus shed His blood by the stripes upon His back, that outward bleeding. He was bruised and battered inside for our iniquity's, wounded inside as well as outwardly for our transgressions. Jesus bled internally from such a severe beating. It is this internal shedding of blood that purges us in the inside of iniquity (repeated sinful ways). Plead the internal blood of Jesus in your spouse's body, that the blood of Jesus shed internally for their iniquities and transgressions flow through their bodies purging them of all sin. Washing them internally, their hearts, their spirit, their souls, of all sin, and making them clean, as white as snow.

Jesus, out of the severe beatings He underwent also suffered from many internal injuries. This was to liberate us from the power of iniquity and transgressions. He had internal wounds and bruises. The bloodshed within was to liberate us from the power of transgressions and iniquities so we can a life free life of curses. Those generational and ancestral curses must go in Jesus name! And now any breach in our physical, emotional and spiritual can also be healed. Hallelujah!

A transgression is something that you do with full knowledge that it is a wrong thing to do. It is willful sin.

Iniquity is a weakness or fault you were born with. For example example, your mother had anger, your grandmother had it, and so do you. It is a generational sin that is handed over. For example, Abraham had a lying problem, so did Isaac and so did Jacob. Jesus came to break the hold of these from us.

4. **He shed blood when they put the crown of thorns on His head.**
   Jesus shed blood through His head when they placed the crown of thorns on His head.

   - "let this mind be in you which was also in Christ Jesus"

Verse where it happened: Mat 27:29 "And plaiting a crown of thorns, they put it on His head, and a reed in His right hand. And they bowed the knee before Him and mocked Him, saying, Hail, King of the Jews!"

Crown of Thorns – Jesus won back our "Prosperity"

Jesus' crown of thorns was placed on Jesus' brow, to break the curse of poverty and release me into God's abundance. Genesis 3:17, 18 2 Corinthians 8,9

   - Gen. 3:17-19 – (The curse of poverty that came upon mankind because of 'Adam' s sin.)

- John 19:2 – And the soldiers twisted a crown of thorns and put it on His head …"

- 2 Cor. 8:9- For you know the grace of our Lord Jesus Christ, yet for your sakes He became poor; that you through His poverty you might become rich.

John 19:2 And the soldiers platted a crown of thorns, and put it on his head, and they put on him a purple robe,

Picture this, a crown being shoved down upon Jesus' head. The blood running down into His eyes and ears. Those thorns so long and thick piercing his head, that if it were not for His skull, they may have pierced into His brain. Apply the blood from the crown of thorns of Jesus over your spouse's eyes, ears and mind, that they be opened to the truth of His word and act on it, Pierce the minds of our spouses with the blood of Jesus shed from those thorns. *(Larry Huchk also make reference about the thorns being a curse on finances, although I think of and use these bleedings in the sense of cleansing of the spirit in prayer and pleading the blood, the blood was shed for all areas of our lives, and can be used over all areas of our lives. Larry Huch is an American non-denominational pastor and televangelist. He is the founder and senior pastor of DFW New Beginnings in Bedford, Texas along with his wife Tiz)*

The Crown of Thorns placed on Jesus head to wound him and mock Him won back your prosperity. Gen. 3: 17-19 God said to Adam and Eve "because you have heeded the voice of your wife, and have eaten from the tree of which I commanded you, saying, "you shall not eat of it." Cursed is the ground for your sake; in toil, you shall eat of it all the days of your life. Both thorns and thistles it shall bring forth for you, and you shall eat the herb of the fields. In the sweat of your face you shall eat bread till you return to the ground.

For Christians, the crown of thorns is a reminder of two things: (1) Jesus was, and is, indeed a king. One day, the entire universe will bow to Jesus as the "King of kings and Lord of Llords" (Revelation 19:16). What the Roman soldiers meant as a mockery, was in fact a picture of Christ's two roles, first of suffering servant (Isaiah 53), and second of conquering Messiah-King (Revelation 19). (2) Jesus was willing to endure the pain, the insults, and the shame, all on our account. The crown of thorns, and the suffering that went with it, are long gone, and Jesus has now received the crown of which He is worthy. "But we see Him who for a little while was made lower than the angels, namely Jesus, crowned with glory and honor because of the suffering of death, so that by the grace of God He might taste death for everyone" (Hebrews 2:9, emphasis added).

What was redeemed: Our peace of mind and healing from all mental torment.

This was to liberate our minds. The word of God says, 'the chastisement of our peace was UPON Him'. The peace which the enemy took from us, God restored it again in Jesus. Now the enemy does not have to afflict our minds and keep them in bondage anymore. All mental bondage and strongholds were removed from when they pressed the thorns into Jesus' head. He suffered and shed blood from His head so that our minds can be free. I have seen a band tied around the minds of men in the realm of the spirit meant to keep them from making the right decision for their destinies, but as I commanded them to break, they all fell off in Jesus name! Hallelujah!!! Our minds can now be free! Also, you may know: if the enemy can oppress our minds, then he can also control our destinies. By freeing us from all bondage and diseases of the mind, Jesus has also freed our destinies. No sickness, disease, stress or condition of the mind can hold us back to the glory of God.

5. **He shed blood when they pierced His hands.**
   Pierced Hands – Jesus won back Dominion/Authority over "What we Touch".

- Gen. 39:3 – God says, "Everything we put our hands to He will cause us to prosper. "."

- Gen. 1:26-28 – (God made man to be just like Him and gave man authority and dominion over all the earth).

  Jesus' hands were pierced by the nails, to restore total dominion to the works of my hands.

  Genesis 1:26-28 Deut. 28:12-13

- Mk. 16:18 – After Jesus died and rose from the dead before ascending into heaven…. He tells believers of their authority that has been returned to them through His blood shed at the cross…" In My name… they will take up serpents; and if they drink anything deadly, it will by no means hurt them; they will lay hands on the sick, and they will recover."

(I do not find scripture speaking directly of the nailing of His hands and feet to the cross, but only that they crucified Him, which by the custom of crucifixion, it was the practice to do such and known therefore how it was done).

The blood shed from the hands was done so that our hands would prosper in everything we touch. I apply the blood from the hands of Jesus also to the hands of my spouse that his hands may not touch anything of defilement., I wash his hands in the blood of Jesus's hands so that they be clean and purified of uncleanliness.

Verse where it happened: Mat 27:35 "And they crucified Him, dividing His garments, casting a lot; so that it might be fulfilled which was spoken by the prophet, "They parted My garments among them, and they cast a lot for My clothing.""
Jesus shed blood when they drove the nail through His left hand.

- Our left hand is weaker than our right. "Let the weak say I am strong"

Jesus shed blood when they drove the nail through His hands.

- Jesus said, "all power is given unto Me, that which I have I give unto you"

They drove nails into His hands: God had placed all authority in the hands of Adam and Eve. Through their disobedience, they lost their authority. Jesus nail pierced hands bought back your authority. You can lay hands on the sick and they will recover. You can lay hands on your children's pillow and declare that they are going to serve God. Lay hands on your children's school books and over their clothes .... declare that everything I put my hands on will prosper. Why? Because the authority has been returned to our hands through the precious blood of Jesus you can touch your children's clothing and command sickness, disease and destroying power to leave your children.

What was redeemed: power to succeed, prosper and ability to receive spiritual inheritance.

Here, Jesus freed us to receive our inheritance. Until then, we could not receive what is ours because our hands were still defiled by sin. Satan could claim before God that we were not qualified to receive anything and it would be so. When the blood oozed from the palms of Jesus, it was to take away the curse on the work of our hands. Ito take away the sin that was testifying against us and freed us to lift our hands to God in worship. The scriptures speak of lifting 'holy hands' to God. Now we can do that because our hands have been purified through the blood of Jesus. Also, the work of our hands can be blessed because the curse that was on the work of our hands was lifted by His wounded hands. Now everything we do can prosper!

6. **He shed blood when they pierced His feet.**
   Jesus shed blood when they drove the nails through His feet.

   - Eph. 6:15 "And your feet shod with the preparation of the gospel of peace".

- "His name shall be called Wonderful, Counselor, The Mighty God, The everlasting Father, and The Prince of Peace."

Pierced Feet – Jesus won back Dominion/authority over "Places we Walk"

Jesus' feet were nailed to the cross, to restore total dominion in my walk.
Joshua 1:3 Deut. 11:24

- Deut. 11:24 - - "Every place on which the sole of your foot treads shall be yours."

- Mark 16: 15 – After Jesus' death on the cross and His resurrection, but before ascending into heaven, He commands all believers to, "Go into all the world and preach the good news to all creation." Reflection Song: "Overcome" by Jeremy Camp

Verse where it happened: Mat 27:35 "And they crucified Him, dividing His garments, casting a lot; so that it might be fulfilled which was spoken by the prophet, "They parted My garments among them, and they cast a lot for My clothing.""

Roman soldiers drove spikes into his feet: Those pierced feet won back dominion over the places we walk. Man was supposed to be the head and not the tail. Man was supposed to be above only and not beneath. When Adam disobeyed God in the Garden of Eden, he lost dominion and authority, and at that moment, Satan became the god of this world. But through Jesus shed blood, we don't have to be trampled by Satan. Instead, we are to trample him! As believers, you have the authority to walk around your neighborhood and say, "I bind the devil in my neighborhood. I bind drug addicts and dope dealers and I loose the presence of Jesus to save, heal, deliver. Through the blood of Jesus, I demolish the plans of the devil and loose the plans that Jesus has for these people.

What was redeemed: our dominion and authority.

Disobedience (in Adam) led to our loss of dominion, but the shed but of Jesus bought it back for us. Dominion is in the place of our feet. That is where we subject every power that rises against us. Anything that is under your feet is under your power. God says, "Every place that the sole of your foot shall tread upon, that have I given unto you..." (Joshua 1:3). Now we can go and take back our cities, towns, families, destinies, because Jesus has restored us to the place of power over the enemy. Luke 10:19 says "Behold, I give to you authority to tread on serpents and scorpions, and over all the authority of the enemy. And nothing shall by any means hurt you." This is dominion. Through the blood, Jesus shed when they nailed His feet on the cross, our feet have also been cleansed from all manner of defilement and we now able to stand before the enemy, to resist him, and to demand that he gives back what is ours. Hallelujah! I have prayed over the feet of many and as I applied the blood, yokes broke off from them!!! In one instance, I anointed the feet of one of my sons while visiting in his house and immediately the yokes broke and God opened His eyes and showed him some key areas of his life that were locked. But from that moment they were free, and right now he is enjoying an abundant life!

7. **Blood came forth when they pierced his side.**
   Verse where it happened: John 19:34 "But one of the soldiers pierced His side with a lance, and instantly there came out blood and water."
   Jesus shed His blood when they drove a spear into His side

   • Jesus exchanged a spear for a royal scepter for He is The King of Kings and the Lord of Lords.

Pierced Heart – Jesus won back our "Joy"

The spear was thrust through Jesus' side, showing that he died from a broken heart, to heal my broken heart. This also illustrates his giving birth to His bride from His side as did the first Adam with Eve. Luke 4:18 Psalm 147:3 AMP

- John 19:32-34: "Then the soldiers came and broke the legs of the first and of the other who was crucified with Jesus. But when they came to Jesus and saw that He was already dead, they did not break His legs. But one of the soldiers pierced His side with a spear, and immediately blood and water came out."

- Neh. 8:10 – The joy of the Lord is your strength.

Joh 7:38 He that believeth on me, as the scripture hath said, out of his belly shall flow rivers of living water.

When the soldier shoved a spear into His side and blood and was poured out; at that moment, he atoned (paid the price) for the brokenhearted to be healed. Neh. 8:10 "The joy of the Lord is your strength." Jesus not only took your sin, but He took the pain of that sin. As the old saying goes, "He'll turn our hurts into halos and our scars into stars." Jesus knows what it is to suffer a broken heart, not only physically in His death on the cross but also through the betrayal and rejection by the very ones He came to love and call friends. Many of those He had ministered to cried, "Crucify Him!"

Jesus' Bruises won our Deliverance from Inner Hurts and Iniquities: If you have a bruise on your body, it means you are bleeding on the inside. Some bruises last a long time and go very deep. Jesus said, "not only will I forgive what they've done on the outside, but I'm going to give them power on the inside so they can walk in total victory.
An iniquity is a bend in our nature to sin as our ancestors did, or a wicked act of sin. That spirit of iniquity tries to break us down. It is a spiritual force on the inside that pressures us to bow or bend under its destructive nature. If you have a deep bruise inside, perhaps from divorce, or suicidal tendencies, or bruises from sexual abuse. Jesus bore your hurts and bruises so that you could be whole again.

What was redeemed: wholeness of heart and fullness of joy.

Jesus went through great heartbreak right from the moment He entered into Jerusalem. First, He was rejected and betrayed by Judas, then the crowd before Pilate also rejected and refused Him preferring Barnabas to be given to them, then He saw His mother watch Him while naked on the cross, then He felt abandoned by the Father too when He cried, 'My God, My God, why hast thou forsaken me?' Betrayal, grief, abandonment, rejection… these are things which gripped the heart of the Master and caused Him much anguish even as He hung on the cross. It was not easy. It is medically proved that a high level of agony can cause water to collect around the heart.

When Jesus died, the soldiers did not pierce His heart, only His side. But when they did, blood and water came out, showing that he literally died of a broken heart. When Jesus first begun His ministry, He said God has sent Him to 'heal the brokenhearted'. So beloved, the enemy may have done many things to crush your heart and will to live, you may have gone through many things at the hands of men, but when we come to Jesus broken hearts are made new again. I remember some time back God spoke to me and said, 'I, the Lord, do not mend; I make all things new'.

Beloved, regardless of what has been done against you by anyone to break your heart, the heart of Jesus was broken so that yours can be made whole again. Broken not by the spear, but by **the anguish,** and the blood that came from there was to make your heart whole again. You can have a brand-new heart from the Master today. You can have your joy restored again. No more sad and gloomy and depressed days, for joy has been repurchased back for you! But, why blood and water? The water likewise cleanses the defiled water in our bodies. The evil water that has been passed to us from generation to generation is broken as the water from the body of Christ now purifies and fills our lives. Now the enemy can defile our bodies no more; we are cleansed! Hallelujah!!!

And of course, with all said and done, Jesus said 'IT IS FINISHED'. He showed that the work of redeeming mankind was completed. Now man could be restored back to God. The curtain in the temple was ripped from top to bottom. A new and a living way had been made into the holiest, a new way through the breaking of the body of Christ, through His blood. Now we may boldly approach the throne of the Father and obtain mercy and find grace to help us in our times of need. What a good God! What a loving Savior! What a great work of redemption! What manner of great restoration! What great freedom has been purchased for us; and that only through THE BLOOD OF JESUS.

This blood that was shed on the cross will never lose its power. Now we are not just restored to what we lost in the Garden of Eden (Adam's state as Son of God) but we are given another second nature; we are fashioned after Jesus' state as Son of God. We are not of the order of the first Adam anymore, but of the second, raised from the dead, and with glorious power! Think about Jesus where He is right now. How glorious do you imagine Him to be? This is the same state God has elevated you to.

But some may say, 'How come I do not look like this?' See this verse: 1 John 3:2 'Beloved, now we are children of God, and it has not yet been revealed what we shall be. But we know that when He shall be revealed, we shall be like Him, for we shall see Him as He is.' Also 1 John 4:17 tells us '…as He is, so also we are in this world.' It may not seem so in the physical beloved, but in the spiritual, we are glorious!!! And the day comes when it shall be as much physical as it is now spiritually, AMEN!

Recap

Seven Places Jesus Shed His Blood:

1. In Gethsemane, Jesus Won Back Our Willpower

2. The Stripes on Jesus' Back Won Back Our Health

3. Jesus' Crown of Thorns Won Back Our Prosperity

4. Jesus' Pierced Hands Won Back Dominion over the Things We Touch

5. Jesus' Pierced Feet Won Back Dominion over the Places We Walk

6. Jesus' Pierced Heart Won Back Our Joy

7. Jesus' Bruises Won Our Deliverance from Inner Hurts and Iniquities

God is the same yesterday, today and tomorrow. When I think of this and all that Jesus did to redeem us from the curse of Adam, I sometime feel that I am living far under the awareness of the provision that He purchased for me at great cost. It cost Him His life, it will certainly cost me mine. (my rights!!) His life is far better than anything that this world could give me. Jesus has overcome this world and all its weaknesses of sin, sickness, and disease. His life in me is resurrection power available to Him as He so chooses to glorify Himself.

"The 7 places Jesus Shed His Blood" Larry Huch

1. Garden of Gethsemane – The first -place Jesus shed his blood was in the Garden of Gethsemane and at this time He won back our will power that Adam lost in the Garden of Eden. Jesus said, "not My Will Lord but Thy will be done".

2. The whipping post –The second-place Jesus shed His blood was at the whipping post. Jesus was flogged 39 times for all disease." "for by His stripes we are healed".

3. Crown of Thorns – The third-place Jesus shed his blood was when the soldiers placed a crown of thorns on His head. This redeemed us from the curse of poverty.

4. From His hands – When the spikes were driven into his hands. Everything we put our hands to God will cause to prosper because of this.

5. His feet – When the spikes were driven through His feet this blood redeemed us from our loss of dominion and authority.

6. His side – When the soldier shoved a spear into His side to be sure He was dead this blood flowed forth from His broken heart and won back our joy.

7. His bruises – The seventh place His blood was shed was His bruises. (A bruise bleeds under the skin) He was bruised for our iniquities. He went to the gates of hell and took back the keys to the kingdom to break the curse of iniquity over us.

~ 7 ~

The Crucifixion... The Way God Sees it

Jesus knew his assignment before he came to the earth. He said I come to seek and save that which is lost. He knew this in eternity in timelessness before he showed up in time. Isaiah 53:2 starts out by saying, "He shall grow up as a tender plant". He said that in the future tense. Isaiah 53:3 says, *"He is despised and rejected of men a man of sorrow acquainted with grief."* In the Hebrew and Aramaic, He said this in present tense. Vs 4 says, *"Surely he has born our griefs and carried our sorrows."* This was said in past tense. When Jesus died on the cross he covered the past, present and the future.

The gospel of Jesus Christ, as we have heard it taught and as we have studied through symmetric truths is involved in six steps: crucified, dead, buried, quickened raised and seated. These are called the six steps to the throne and are taken from I Kings 10:18-19, that tells us that Solomon's throne had six steps to it. King Solomon is a type or pictures King Jesus. There were six steps to King Solomon's throne. This is a physical illustration a spiritual truth. The six steps to the throne consist of the six things Jesus did and the six things it means to you. The first three steps - crucified, dead and buried, these do away with our old man; they do away with who we used to be. The other three steps - quickened, raised and seated, these are who we are now. With that in mind, let's look at our six steps and remember that every step has a riser and every step has a tread. The six risers are the things that Jesus did and the six treads is what it means to you. What is true of Christ is true of us also. We are going to look through the scriptures and look for the word with. The reason we are looking for the word with is that it tells us when it happened to us.

Six Steps to the Throne

> *Galatians 2:20 "I am crucified with Christ: nevertheless, I live; yet not I, but Christ liveth in me: and the life which I now live in the flesh I live by the faith of the Son of God, who loved me, and gave himself for me."*

1. **Crucified** – We know that Christ was crucified on the cross. The verse says that we were crucified with Christ. This didn't happen in your natural body. Ephesians 5 says that no man ever hated his own flesh. This happened in the spirit over 2000 years ago. Jesus was crucified and we were crucified with him in the spirit. It is not I that lives because I was crucified. We are now the body of Christ and we have His nature. What is living is not I, but Christ living in me.

   > *Romans 6:6 Knowing this, that our old man is crucified with him, that the body of sin might be destroyed, that henceforth we should not serve sin.*

As we see, we were crucified when He was crucified and now since we are the body of Christ, Adam would be the body of sin. This isn't something that you can do now; it's something that has already been done. The body of sin was destroyed. The scripture said He was made to be sin. That's when the body of sin was destroyed; it was destroyed in Him. We used to be part of the body of Adam or the body of sin, now we are part of the body of Christ. We need to understand that our old man was crucified with Christ. God is not fixing us up; he did away with our old man, of who we used to be. The trip to the cross was a one-way ticket... and your old man didn't come back. A new creation was revealed in the resurrection of Christ.

2. **Died** – The next process after being crucified with Christ is that you died.

   > *2 Corinthians 5:14 "For the love of Christ constraineth us; because we thus judge, that if one died for all (the Law of*

> *the Substitutionary Lamb), then were all dead (The Law of Identification):"*

The judgment we come to is that is has already been done. You will always fear judgment until you realize that you've been judged in Him/Christ. The cross was a legal transaction, when Jesus died for us, we all died. Our old man is dead. We are not trying to kill him off, he is already dead. His death was our death. We died with Christ. In John 12, Jesus said, "And I, if I be lifted up from the earth, will draw all men unto me." This is not talking about praise and worship. Jesus died the death of every man – past, present and future. God sees the death of Jesus as our death. He opened up his pure and lovely spirit and took in our lying, our backbiting, our cursing, our gambling and every other sin – past, present and future. You were part of the crucifixion. Not only were you there, but you were also hanging up on the cross. The scripture in John goes on to say, "This he said, signifying what death he should die." You may ask, what death did you die Jesus? He died the death of every man. This includes every man, woman, boy and girl that has been born and yet to be born. This is an Amazing Grace.

> *Romans 6:10 "For in that he died, he died unto sin once: but in that he liveth, he liveth unto God."*

Not only has He dealt in time but he also deals in timelessness. Time ends but God never ends. When you have children, God will cover them. All they have to do is confess that Jesus died for them. Jesus was so radical that he changed BC to AD. He changed time altogether. If we reckon ourselves to be dead, then we don't have a sin problem. Plus, he who is forgiven much loveth much. You are not an old sinner saved by Grace. This type of thinking keeps you sin conscious. He that is dead is free from sin. Your old man has been killed off. Religion would have you think that you escaped death, but you didn't. We got everything we deserved. Nowhere in the bible does it record that you escaped death. Colossians 3:3 "For ye are dead and your life is hid with Christ in God."

3. **Buried** – After someone dies, they are buried. That is exactly what happened to us.

> *Colossians 2:12-13 Buried with him in baptism, wherein also ye are risen with him through the faith of the operation of God, who hath raised him from the dead.13 And you, being dead in your sins and the uncircumcision of your flesh, hath he quickened together with him, having forgiven you all trespasses;*

We were buried when He was buried. You must get a revelation of this and know that the old man is dead and has been buried. He was put in the tomb, so stop digging him up and bringing him to church.

> *Romans 5:8 "But God commendeth his love toward us, in that, while we were yet sinners, Christ died for us"*

The love of God is the only love that the church will ever be fulfilled with. It was His love that was expressed at the cross of Calvary as He became one with us. While we were yet sinners, He chose to be in union with us. Jesus became exactly who and what we were, so much so that when God saw Him, He saw us. This is the Law of Identification. Identify means to consider or treat as the same. God identified us with Christ on the cross. Jesus became exactly who we were and there God vindicated his wrath upon us in Christ. Jesus was never guilty of anything. We were the ones guilty of sin. Jesus became so much like whom we were that God legally saw Christ as being us. In the garden of Gethsemane, Jesus said, Father, if thou be willing, remove this cup from me. He said this because he had never been separated from His Father and he was about to take on the entire sinful nature of mankind. He was about to become who we were. Jesus didn't die instead of you, he died as you. He died as everything you don't like about you and everything God didn't like about you. He opened up his pure and lovely spirit to become one with fallen humanity in order to produce a righteous people.

4. **Quickened** – Quicken means to be made alive. We were quickened together with Christ.

> *Ephesians 2:5 "Even when we were dead in sins, hath quickened us together with Christ, (by grace ye are saved;)"*

After three days in the tomb the Holy Spirit entered the dead body of Jesus as the son of man and gave Him life, the God-kind-of-life, eternal life and that life quickened Him. We were "quickened together with" Christ. In order for us to be quickened together with Him, we had to be dead together with Him.

> *I Peter 3:18 "For Christ also hath once suffered for sins, the just for the unjust, that he might bring us to God, being put to death in the flesh, but quickened by the Spirit:"*

> *The same kind of life that Jesus received is available to us when we are born of the Spirit of God.*

5. **Raised** – After three days, Christ rose from the dead. Since we are in Him, we were resurrected with him and now we have resurrected life.

> *Ephesians 2: 6 And hath raised us up together, and made us sit together in heavenly places in Christ Jesus:*

> *Colossians 3:1 If ye then be risen with Christ, seek those things which are above, where Christ sitteth on the right hand of God.*

Jesus became who we were when he went in that tomb, but he came out different. Who we were didn't come out of the tomb. Jesus became the last Adam. He became the federal head of the "new creation" of mankind. When He was raised from the dead is when He became the head of this body. Christ is the new man that creates in himself a new creation and body of believers who partake of his divine nature. Just as He was raised a new creation man, so were we. We get his life because we are in Him that has life. We are in-Christer. God was giving life to us in Him when he raised Jesus from the dead. Therefore we have that resurrected life and we are a new creature in Christ.

6. **Seated** - After Jesus was raised, He ascended to be seated in heavenly places and is now sitting at the right hand of the father. Ephesians 2:6 says that we sit together in heavenly places in Christ. Because we are believers, our seating with Christ is part of our inheritance now. This is where we are already seated, because when Jesus was seated in triumph, we were seated with Him. When Jesus sat down at the right hand of the Father, we sat down with Him far above principalities and powers. Our position and seating in Christ is a fact. It has already happened. When we get the revelation of what happened to us in Christ on the cross and our position in Christ, we will get the understanding that we are in the one who rules and reigns and that we can walk in that authority.

If you understand the six steps to the throne, then you understand that everything Jesus did, He did for us. When he died for us, He died as us. He didn't die "instead of" us; He didn't die "in place of" us; if he had died in place of us then we wouldn't be changed. Most people believe Jesus died instead of them, so they never grow up in Him. They don't expect to actually display His glory as the body of Christ.

Ecclesiastes 3:14-15 I know that, whatsoever God doeth, it shall be for ever: nothing can be put to it, nor any thing taken from it: and God doeth it, that men should fear before him. ¹⁵ That which hath been is now; and that which is to be hath already been; and God requireth that which is past.

Whatever God does it is forever. The devil can't take your salvation. Whatever God does, no one can take it from you. This is why Romans 8:35 says, *"Who shall separate us from the Love of God? Shall tribulation, or distress, or persecution, or famine, or nakedness, or peril, or sword?"* Nothing and no one can pluck you out of the Father's hand. There are some sins that you might do that might come up, but the blood of Jesus will cover your imperfect soul and corrupt body. Thank God for the blood of Jesus, it will never lose its power. You have an incorruptible seed on the inside of you because you are born again even though you are in a corruptible world. Whatever God does it shall be forever. You can rest in that. Ecclesiastes 3:14 goes on to say, *Nothing, can be put to it nor anything taken from it. God doeth it that men shall be in awe before him.*

Verse 15 says, "That which is been is now." This happened in the mind of God before time began. That which is to be hath already been. In heaven, in the beginning where there was no time this was talked about around the tables of eternity. It says, that which is past because he stated that which would be before he created time. He stated in his mind what would be and then created a space called time to play out what was already in his mind. Jesus already knew that he was going to the cross and that he would go to the lost sheep of Israel first. He knew that Israel would reject him and he would turn to the Gentiles. It's called bible prophecy. Zechariah 9:9 says, Jesus would come riding in on a donkey and that's exactly what happened. People have a tendency of saying time will tell. I tell you time doesn't tell. Time unfolds what eternity has already told. God knows everything from the beginning to the end. He is the author and the finisher of our faith. Our life is already planned out.

It is the Event of Tenses and Times: Past, Present and Future. No sin and no events are beyond His power to touch and redeem. When He died on the cross he covered everything. He covered your growing up, getting old, divorces, fornicating, lying. He covered everything. The cross was a legal transaction. God does everything legally. That is why the bible says in *Romans 8:33, "Who can lay anything to the charge of God's elect?"* You can't be charged because whatsoever God does is forever. God loves you all the way through eternity. He loved us before we even came here. He knew us in His bosom. We all lived in the bosom of God before we came here. The world is a spiritual world. You don't have a spirit; you are a spirit, encased in a body, with a soul. When you got born- again, God perfected your spirit. Your spirit is perfect. The end of Heb. 12:23 say, to the spirits of just men made perfect. Your spirit is perfect. What God is working on now is your soul - the way you think, want and feel and you learning how to keep your body under subjection. This is a lifetime process. That is what the blood is for. The blood is not for your spirit because your spirit is perfect. You mess up in your soul, the way you think, want and feel and your body. So you have to confess it and plead the blood over it. You don't need to plead the blood over a perfect spirit. God made your spirit perfect. He made what was just like him perfect. But your body is not perfect. God saves your spirit and then tells you that he is going to work out your soul salvation through you perfect spirit by the working of the Holy Spirit, as we have learned salvation is progressive: saved (spirit), soul (being saved) and body (shall be saved). *II Corinthians 1:10 "Who delivered us from so great a death, and doth deliver: in whom we trust that he will yet deliver us".*

For the love of God is not bound by time. It is time that is bound by love. God took the past, present and future and spread his love all the way across it through eternal redemption. God is not bound by time. Your sins are already covered in the future. Love can extend the intentions of time. God says I can extend my love in the past, present and future and cover all of your sins. For love covers a multitude of sins. Love can extend the intentions of time because time will be swallowed up in eternity. Love is God's motivation because God is love. The greatest of these is love. Love changed the intentions of time and has covered our future sins because the cross was a legal transaction outside of time done in the spirit in the perfect tense. It is a finished work. So Jesus died the death of all men in the spirit. You are a spirit, with a soul encased in a body.

II Corinthians says 5:17 reads, "Therefore if any man be in Christ, he is a new creature: old things are passed away; behold, all things are become new."

If you are born again then you are a new creature in Christ. The person you used to be doesn't exist anymore. He was crucified, and then he died and was buried. Your new creation was quickened, raised and is now seated in heavenly places. What is being worked on now is the way we think (intellect), want (desires) and feel (emotions). We have to do two things which are to afflict our soul and renew our mind. The incorruptible seed is in you. The incorruptible seed is Jesus and we received Him in seed form when we became born again. When you come to church you get the seed watered and that seed grows up all over you. The incorruptible seed (Jesus) is in us which liveth and abideth forever (I Peter 1:23).

ᖇ *8* ᖇ

What did Jesus Do for those three days?

Matthew 12:40 (KJV) For as Jonas was three days and three nights in the whale's belly; so, shall the Son of man be three days and three nights in the heart of the earth.

In the previous chapter, we saw the events surrounding the crucifixion of Jesus Christ. We also saw those that witnessed the events on that historic day. The chapter ends with a massive celebration on the part of Lucifer and all his cohorts. On the other side, we had all of heaven in total silence. They were all in total awe and shock at the horrendous events and sights that they had just witnessed.

The scene shifts to Hades; the place of the unrighteous dead.

IMPORTANT NOTE

What is a parable?

A parable (noun) is a simple story used to illustrate a moral or spiritual lesson, as told by Jesus in the Gospels.

When Jesus spoke to the people, He often spoke in parables. When He spoke in parables no names are ever mentioned, because they were illustrations. However, on other occasions, He told true stories. The passage we are about to discuss is certainly a true story since it names one of the participants.

1 Peter 3:18-19 NIV
[18] For Christ died for sins once for all, the righteous for the unrighteous, to bring you to God. He was put to death in the body but made alive by the Spirit,

[19] through whom also he went and preached to the spirits in prison...

Now it is important to understand what this means. We can get two very good clues.

The first clue is found in what the Jews believed about Hades. They believed that Hades was broken into two compartments. One compartment which they called Paradise is where the believers went when they died. Paradise is the place where the righteous dead were.

The second compartment was where non-believers went when they died. This place is the place of the unrighteous dead. They believed that both compartments were in the bowels of the earth.

Jesus tell this story:
(Luke 16:19-26 NIV)
19 "There was a rich man who was dressed in purple and fine linen and lived in luxury every day.
20 At his gate was laid a beggar named Lazarus, covered with sores
21 and longing to eat what fell from the rich man's table. Even the dogs came and licked his sores.
22 "The time came when the beggar died and the angels carried him to Abraham's side. The rich man also died and was buried.
23 In hell, where he was in torment, he looked up and saw Abraham far away, with Lazarus by his side.
24 So he called to him, 'Father Abraham, have pity on me and send Lazarus to dip the tip of his finger in water and cool my tongue, because I am in agony in this fire.'
25 "But Abraham replied, 'Son, remember that in your lifetime you received your good things, while Lazarus received bad things, but now he is comforted here and you are in agony.
26 And besides all this, between us and you a great chasm has been fixed, so that those who want to go from here to you cannot, nor can anyone cross over from there to us.'

Jesus Descended into Hell

Jesus had to pay the penalty for our sins., This would have included not only His tasting death for every man **(Hebrews 2:9 - But we see Jesus, who was made a little lower than the angels for the suffering of death, crowned with glory and honor; that he by the grace of God should taste death for every man.)**, for the wages of sin is death. But it would have included His descending into hell, the place where all sinners deserve to go. The Apostles' Creed states it this way: "He descended into hell." Scripture gives us some hints to show that in hell Christ was conscious after His death on the cross and that His performance in hell was an important part of His earthly ministry. Peter, mentions the crucified Christ in **Acts 2:24 - Whom God hath raised up, having loosed the pains of death: because it was not possible that he should be holden of** it. Two things are implied in this verse:
1. that death exerted "pains"
2. that something called "death" tried so hard to hold Him that God Himself had to intervene.

Clearly there was a titanic struggle going on those three days. During this awful battle, several things took place. There was punishment for our sins. Christ took on Himself the guilt of the human race, including its worst crimes. In God's sight, Christ was "made sin." His whole being reeked with our sin. The sin had to be punished. Punishment for sin required more than a physical death. If punishment consisted merely of separating spirit from body, which physical death does, then Christ could have almost instantly revived after three o'clock that awful afternoon and sped back to His Father. Punishment for sin follows physical death.

I Peter 3:18,19 - For Christ also hath once suffered for sins, the just for the unjust, that he might bring us to God, being put to death in the flesh, but quickened by the Spirit: By which also he went and preached unto the spirits in prison; This verse indicates He carried on activities which show He was alive and fully aware of His mission there. And, as He predicted, He was "three days and three nights in the heart of the earth," not just in the garden tomb **(Matthew 12:40).**

Christ received the same type of punishment the rich man in **Luke 16** experienced, cut off from God and godly men, abandoned to the torments of bell fire, and gloated over by Satan. It is the horror awaiting every Christ rejecter. When Jesus said in the garden, "if it be possible for this cup to pass. **" Mark 14:35,36 - And he went forward a little, and fell on the ground, and prayed that, if it were possible, the hour might pass from him. And he said, Abba, Father, all things are possible unto thee; take away this cup from me: nevertheless, not what I will, but what thou wilt.** Thus, it was the prospect of what went beyond his unspeakable death - the spikes, the nakedness, the sun's heat, the flies, the spitting, the jeering, the wracking of His body in hideous pain. It was the horrible, black anguish of the coming guilt of our sins and the fear of His Father's rejection. Surely, this was the bitterest drop in the cup. He who had seen from before the foundation of the world what awaited any spirit delivered to "him who has the power of death, that is the devil," knew full well the horror that lurked for Him the moment He passed through "the gates of Hades."

Many of the gloating spirits that animated all Hades as Jesus descended may be guessed at from His parable of the vineyard where wicked servants, having killed a succession of prophets, said to each other, "This is the heir. Come, let us kill Him and take His inheritance" **(Matthew 21:38 - But when the husbandmen saw the son, they said among themselves, this is the heir; come, let us kill him, and let us seize on his inheritance).** Surely this is what Satan had in mind. If somehow, he could incarcerate Jesus, then the earth's inheritance would be his. Every sinner is Satan's prey; here is Christ - with all our sins, and in Satan's sight the greatest sinner of all, forsaken by God and assigned to "taste of death for every man." Satan determined His punishment would be full measure.

Scripture does not tell us what "the pains of death" were like, but it does say that God "loosed" them. Hell's handcuffs were snapped on Christ and its gates clang shut behind Him. For over four thousand years no sinful human soul had ever escaped that prison. The "gulf" was "fixed" too deep and wide for any transition **(Luke 16:25,26 - But Abraham said, Son, remember that thou in thy lifetime receiveth thy good things, and likewise Lazarus evil things: but now he is comforted, and thou art tormented. And beside all this, between us and you there is a great gulf fixed: so that they which would pass from hence to you cannot; neither can they pass to us, that would come from thence).**

Here was Christ - all alone. "I looked, and there was none to help, and I wondered that there was none to uphold" **(Isaiah 63:5 - And I looked, and there was none to help; and I wondered that there was none to uphold: therefore, mine own arm brought salvation unto me; and my fury, it upheld me).** No angel was there, except hell's angels. For the first time in all eternity the Son of God was alone. Yet not entirely.

Here is when God shows up and shows out. My Friend, there comes a time in all our lives when we feel alone, **2 Corinthians 4:8-10 (KJV).**

8 We are troubled on every side, yet not distressed; we are perplexed, but not in despair;

9 Persecuted, but not forsaken; cast down, but not destroyed;

10 Always bearing about in the body the dying of the Lord Jesus, that the life also of Jesus might be made manifest in our body.

The Holy Spirit - the Paraclete (He who stands besides us) was still with Him. It was "through the eternal Spirit" that He "offered Himself without blemish unto God". **(Hebrews 9:14 - How much more shall the blood of Christ, who through the eternal Spirit offered himself without spot to God, purge**

your conscience from dead works to serve the living God)? It was this faithful companion who plumbed with Christ the depths of Hell. He empowered the Savior's arm for combat, and the outcome is described as follows in **Colossians 2:15 - And having spoiled principalities and powers, he made a shew of them openly, triumphing over them in it.** These principalities are infernal, not heavenly. They represent Satan's most potent warriors. Christ took them on in their own den and despoiled them. He stripped them, threw them down, and left them impotent. These evil beings are immobilized, not annihilated. Christ subjected them with His God-given power. **Philippians 2:9,10 - Wherefore God also hath highly exalted him, and given him a name which is above every name: That at the name of Jesus every knee should bow, of things in heaven, and things in earth, and things under the earth.**

It was this combat in hell that "brought to naught" Satan's power over humanity. Satan must live to witness the absolute triumph of Christ over all creation.

Now, Jesus makes His way to Satan's throne room for another encounter. As Satan invaded the Garden of Eden to deceive Adam and Eve. Jesus invaded Satan's domain. Jesus had to undo what Lucifer set in motion in the Garden of Eden.

Let's see what occurred in the Garden to get a better understanding to what Jesus was about to do.

God Gave Authority to Man

Genesis 1:26-27 NIV *Then God said, "Let us make man in our image, in our likeness, and let them rule over the fish of the sea and the birds of the air, over the livestock, over all the earth, and over all the creatures that move along the ground." So, God created man in his own image, in the image of God he created him; male and female he created them.*

It was as simple as that. God armed humanity with authority over all creatures and earth itself. God gave mankind **dominion** over the earth to rule it. The earth still belonged to God, but it was for man to rule. God, the ultimate **ruler and authority of all things**, gave humanity its own little corner of creation to rule. When God establishes an issue, it is established. Just as creation is bound to follow the natural laws established by God, God follows His Own Laws. Since God is ultimately righteous, God's word is ultimately true. God cannot go back on His word, because to deny His word would be to deny His authority, which establishes His word as truth.

God began humanity with the man, Adam and his wife, Eve. God lived in close communion with the two; enjoying walks in the garden with them, talking with them, just spending time together. God loved them and they returned love to God. More importantly, they obeyed their loving Father. God told them not to eat of the tree of the knowledge of good and evil and they didn't. As long as they obeyed the Father, they enjoyed His presence and company.

But there was trouble brewing in the garden. In chapter three of the book of Genesis, it tells the story of how Satan, in the form of a serpent, deceived Eve and she ate of the tree of the knowledge of good and evil. Eve then had her husband to eat the fruit also. In their act of disobedience to the only law God gave them, Adam and Eve cut themselves off from communion with the Father. In eating of the fruit a transference took place, Adam and Eve abdicated the authority, power and dominion that Jesus had given them at their creation. In exchange, Satan imparted his nature into them. Mankind has had to deal with the Sin Nature ever since. The only way to regain abdicated power and authority is through confrontation.

JESUS INVADES SATAN'S LAIR

Jesus then approaches Satan's throne room for the confrontation to regain that which was lost in the Garden of Eden. I can just picture Jesus grabbing Satan by the collar and saying "I Am here to take back what rightfully belongs to me". Matthew

28:18 And Jesus came and spake unto them, saying, "All power is given unto me in heaven and in earth." As Jesus takes what rightfully belongs to Him. Jesus deposits back into Satan all the sins of the world (the place of their origin). **HALLELUJAH!!!!!, Hallelujah to the Lamb!!!!!**

JESUS MAKES HIS WAY TO PARADISE

Jesus divested Himself of the sins that He took upon Himself at the cross. This now gives Jesus the right to go to Paradise **(The place of the righteous dead)** as He promised the penitent thief.

Jesus promised that "this day you shall be with me in paradise". There are many that believe that Jesus spent three days and nights in hell, the place of torment (the place of the unrighteous dead). The words of Jesus Himself should correct the error of false doctrine.

Can you imagine the welcome that Jesus got as He arrived in Paradise? Jesus, the conqueror, has arrived as victor over death, hell and the grave.

Upon arrival in Paradise, Jesus began preaching to all the saints. Can you imagine those present? There was Adam, Noah, Job, Abraham, Isaac, Jacob, Moses, Joshua, King David, Isaiah, Daniel, the three Hebrew boys, Esther, Ruth, Rehab, the penitent thief, etc. The message Jesus preached was that He (Jesus) was the fulfillment of all the messianic prophesies thathad been spoken.

Jesus, began from the beginning of time and preached to the saints that were there of the Fathers, Great Love. That He, Jesus, was God's greatest expression of love to mankind. He reminded Adam of the animals that were slain to cover the shame and sin. He showed them the thorn marks in His head and reminded Abraham of the thorn bush where the rams horns were caught. He reminded Moses that He, Jesus, was the Passover Lamb. He reminded Aaron that He, Jesus was the High Priest. Jesus showed them His scourged back. He showed them His pierced hands and feet. He showed them His pierced side.

My friend, this same Jesus, is still desiring to show Himself to you and I, that he truly loved us to the death. And if we were the only people on earth needing a savior, He would have gladly died for us.

In the next chapter, you will see Jesus at the resurrection.

∽ 9 ∽

The Grave to the Throne

Importance of the Resurrection

The bodily resurrection of Jesus Christ from the dead is crowning proof of Christianity. Everything else that was said or done by Christ and the apostles is secondary in importance to the resurrection.

The Events After the Resurrection of Christ

The four Gospels each contain bits of information about the events occurring after the resurrection of Jesus Christ. Putting the four accounts together provides us with a detailed harmonization.

1. **Christ rises from the dead very early Sunday morning.** A violent earthquake and an angel rolling away the stone and sitting upon it accompany this event. The guards are traumatized because they have seen this angel, and they freeze **(Matthew 28:2-4)**.

2. **Mary Magdalene and another Mary either walk to the tomb** together or they had planned to meet there. When she (or they) arrives, the stone has been rolled away. (The guards are gone by now.) She returns to find Peter and John and tells them that someone has moved Jesus' body **(John 20:1-2; Matthew 28:1)**.

3. **Another group of women were scheduled to meet the two Mary's at the tomb.** They have acquired spices to complete the burial process, which had been hurried. They are concerned about finding some men to help roll

the stone away, since it was large and needed to be rolled against gravity. To their surprise, these women see two angels, only one of which speaks, telling them that Jesus has been raised. The women are scared to death and leave [seeing angels has this effect] **(Mark 16:2-8; Luke 24:1-8, Matthew 28:5-8).**

4. **Peter and John arrive after being summoned by Mary Magdalene,** who apparently follows them there. John looks into the tomb, but Peter goes inside. All he finds are the burial clothes. They return, confused, but Mary Magdalene apparently stays at the tomb to grieve that someone has removed Jesus' body **(Luke 24:12, John 20:3-10).**

5. **Jesus makes His first appearance to Mary Magdalene, after Peter and John have left.** At first she supposes Him to be the gardener, but she is then overjoyed to realize that it is the Lord **(John 20:11-17, Mark 16:9).**

6. **Jesus then appears to these other women** who had left before Peter and John had arrived. These are the women who saw the angels. Jesus tells them to communicate that the disciples were to prepare to travel to Galilee **(Matthew 28:9-10).**

7. **The women, joined by Mary Magdalene, report their meeting with Jesus to the disciples,** but they write it off as nonsense **(Mark 16:10-11, Luke 24:9-11, John 20:18).**

8. **The Roman guards report what they had witnessed to the chief priests.** They were bribed to say that someone stole the body of Jesus while they were asleep. The priests promised the soldiers protection from military discipline through their clout **(Matthew 28:11-15).**

Matt 27 & 28 Jesus Arose and Paradise Emptied

Resurrection Morning

When the first rays of sunlight began to peek over the horizon, several supernatural events began to unfold. The earth that previously convulsed at the time of Jesus death now started reacting to another supernatural occurrence. Jesus stated that in three days he would rise. On that great resurrection morning, the earth began to quake, lightening flashed and two visitors from heaven appeared in a great shaft of light. These two visitors were angels sent by God to roll the stone of the grave away. Jesus did not need them to open the grave to get out, but this was, so mankind could see and know Jesus had risen. He had risen indeed.

In Matthew 28:1-10 (KJV) this event is recorded

1. *In the end of the sabbath, as it began to dawn toward the first day of the week, came Mary Magdalene and the other Mary to see the sepulcher.*
2. *And, behold, there was a great earthquake: for the angel of the Lord descended from heaven, and came and rolled back the stone from the door, and sat upon it.*
3. *His countenance was like lightning, and his raiment white as snow:*
4. *And for fear of him the keepers did shake, and became as dead men.*
5. *And the angel answered and said unto the women, fear not ye: for I know that ye seek Jesus, which was crucified.*
6. *He is not here: for he is risen, as he said. Come, see the place where the Lord lay.*
7. *And go quickly, and tell his disciples that he is risen from the dead; and, behold, he goeth before you into Galilee; there shall ye see him: lo, I have told you.*
8. *And they departed quickly from the sepulcher with fear and great joy; and did run to bring his disciples word.*
9. *And as they went to tell his disciples, behold, Jesus met them, saying, All hail. And they came and held him by the feet, and worshipped him.*

10. Then said Jesus unto them, be not afraid: go tell my brethren that they go into Galilee, and there shall they see me.

The Empty Tomb

The first evidence the disciples had for the resurrection was that of the empty tomb. This evidence is still unanswerable. As Peter and John entered the tomb, they saw an amazing thing. The heavy wrappings of linen clothes which Joseph and Nicodemus had wound around the body of Jesus (John 19:39-40) were still there, just as they had been, but the body had vanished out of them and the grave clothes had, as it were, collapsed inward on themselves. No wonder the record says that when John entered the tomb, "he saw, and believed!" (John 20:8). His doubts and fears immediately gave way to an amazed faith; the collapsed grave clothes yielded no possible interpretation except that the physical body of the crucified Christ had returned to life.In such a remarkable form it could simply pass through the linen wrappings and enter henceforth into the power of an endless life!

The fact that the tomb was empty shows clearly that the resurrection of Christ was a bodily resurrection, not a spiritual resurrection. The latter idea is a self-contradiction, in fact. The spirit does not die and therefore cannot be "resurrected." Indeed, resurrection takes place when the spirit returns to the body from which it has departed.

So powerful is the testimony of the empty tomb that the enemies of Christ had resorted to many strange and wonderful devices to try to explain it away. The first such attempt was the lie that the disciples had stolen the body (Matthew 28:11-15). Such a thing was utterly out of the question, of course. The disciples were hiding in fear for their lives and nothing could have been further from their thoughts than this. Furthermore, the tomb had been sealed, a great stone rolled in front of it, and a watch of Roman soldiers set to guard it (Matthew 27:62-66).

The First Resurrection

As the earth quaked and trembled, and lightening flashed all about, something happened in Paradise.

As Jesus made his way to the grave site, the doors of Paradise opened and yielded all the saints (The Righteous Dead) that had died in the past. These saints went through the streets of Jerusalem declaring the good news (The Gospel of Jesus Christ). These saints were testifying about the death, burial and resurrection of Jesus Christ. Hallelujah to the LAMB!!!!!

We see this account in Matthew 27:52-53 (KJV)
52 And the graves were opened; and many bodies of the saints which slept arose,
53 And came out of the graves after his resurrection, and went into the holy city, and appeared unto many.

Mary Magdalene Sees Jesus

The encounter of Mary Magdalene and Jesus is very important for us to get understanding.

When Jesus arrived at the gravesite, He saw a grieving follower that loved Him dearly. Please do not read anything impure in that statement. As a follower, she loved Him in a platonic way as did Lazarus, Mary and Martha.

When Mary approached the grave weeping, Jesus called out to her, to comfort her. Upon recognizing Jesus voice, Mary was about to embrace Him. This when Jesus made the statement "Mary, touch me not, for I have yet not ascended to the father."

There are several translations that have not translated this properly. The NIV quotes Jesus as saying Mary do not keep on clinging on to me for I have yet not ascended to the Father. This is pure biblical error. Shame on them. This is due to a lack of understanding.

The simple reason that the NIV is incorrect is that when Jesus arose He had already divested Himself of sin while in Hades (the place of the unrighteous dead). Jesus was now without sin. Jesus had not yet ascent to the Father to complete the atonement. Had Mary touched him she would defiled Him and made Him unclean. Thus, rendering his sacrificial work void. Jesus would have to go through the process all over again.

John 20:11-18 (KJV)

11 But Mary stood without at the sepulcher weeping: and as she wept, she stooped down, and looked into the sepulcher,

12 And seeth two angels in white sitting, the one at the head, and the other at the feet, where the body of Jesus had lain.

13 And they say unto her, "Woman, why weepest thou?" She saith unto them, because they have taken away my LORD, and I know not where they have laid him.

14 And when she had thus said, she turned herself back, and saw Jesus standing, and knew not that it was Jesus.

15 Jesus saith unto her, "Woman, why weepest thou? whom seekest thou?" She, supposing him to be the gardener, saith unto him, "Sir, if thou have borne him hence, tell me where thou hast laid him, and I will take him away."

16 Jesus saith unto her, "Mary". She turned herself, and saith unto him, Rabboni; which is to say, Master.

17 Jesus saith unto her," touch me not; for I am not yet ascended to my Father: but go to my brethren, and say unto them, I ascend unto my Father, and your Father; and to my God, and your God."

The Significance of Christ's Resurrection

Each spring, millions of people around the world acknowledge, in some fashion or another, Jesus Christ was raised from the dead some twenty centuries ago. Modern society calls it "Easter."

The origin of this term is uncertain, though it is commonly thought to derive from Eastre, the name of a Teutonic spring goddess. The term "Easter," in the King James Version of the Bible (Acts 12:4), is a mistranslation. The Greek word is pascha, correctly rendered "Passover" in later translations. In fact, though pascha is found twenty-nine times in the Greek New Testament, it is only rendered "Easter" once, even in the KJV.

Christians celebrate Easter as a special annual event acknowledging the resurrection of Christ. Faithful children of God reflect upon the Savior's resurrection **every Sunday** (the resurrection day John 20:1) as they gather to worship God in the regular assembly of the church (Acts 20:7; 1 Corinthians 16:2).

The resurrection of Jesus from the dead is the foundation of the Christian system (cf. 1 Corinthians 15:14ff). If there was no resurrection, Christianity is a hoax. We are wasting our time. But the truth is, the event of Jesus' resurrection is incontrovertible. Professor Thomas Arnold of Rugby, a world-renowned historian, once said that Christ's resurrection from the dead is the "best-attested fact in human history" (1939, 2569). This being the case, just what is the significance of Jesus' resurrection? Think about these matters.

First, the resurrection is one of the major evidences that Jesus Christ is **the Son of God**. Paul affirmed that Christ is "declared to be the Son of God with power.. by the resurrection from the dead" (Romans 1:4).

Second, Jesus' resurrection represents an assurance that we can have **forgiveness from our** sins. Paul contended: "[I]f Christ hath not been raised, our faith is vain; ye are yet in your sins" (1 Cor. 15:17). The reverse of the apostle's affirmation would be this: if Jesus was raised, sins will be forgiven when we obey the gospel (Acts 2:38; 22:16).

Third, the resurrection tells the world that **the kingdom of God is ruled by a living sovereign**. The founder of Islam is dead and his bones lie dormant in the earth. But the founder of Christianity—sixty years after his death—appeared to John on the island of Patmos and said: "I am the first and the last, and the living one; and I was dead, and behold, I am alive for evermore" (Rev. 1:17-18).

Fourth, Jesus' resurrection proves that **physical death is not the termination of human existence**. God, who is the giver of life (1 Tim. 6:13), has the power to reanimate the human body. Christ's triumph over the grave is Heaven's pledge to us that we too shall be raised. This is why Jesus is referred to as the "first fruits of them that are asleep" (1 Corinthians 15:20,23).

Fifth, the Lord's resurrection previewed the **ultimate victory of Christianity over all its enemies**. In the book of Revelation, Jesus is depicted as a lamb that had been slain, but was standing again (5:6). This same Lord was "the lion of the tribe of Judah" that had overcome his foes (5:5). Christians too will overcome as a result of the Lamb's sacrifice and victory over death (cf. Rev. 12:11).

The resurrection of the Son of God should be a constant reminder to us of these wonderful biblical truths. We honor our Master's victory over death—not once a year, but every week!

No wonder then, in view of the combined evidences of the empty tomb, the numerous appearances, the change in the disciples, and the authenticity of the records, not to mention the testimony of two thousand years of Christian history, that such a man as Thomas Arnold, formerly Professor of History at Rugby and Oxford, one of the world's great historians, could say:

"I know of no one fact in the history of mankind which is proved by better, fuller evidence of every sort, to the understanding of a fair inquirer, than the great sign which God hath given us that Christ died, and rose again from the dead."[1]

In like manner, Simon Greenleaf, one of the most skilled legal minds ever produced in this nation, top authority on the question of what constitutes sound evidence, developer of the Harvard Law School, after a thorough evaluation of the four

Gospel accounts from the point of view of their validity as objective testimonial evidence, concluded:

"It was therefore impossible that they could have persisted in affirming the truths they had narrated, had not Jesus actually risen from the dead, and had they not known this fact as certainly as they knew any other fact."[2]

It is no exaggeration, therefore, to maintain that the bodily resurrection of Christ is as certain as any fact of history can ever be. If there is anything at all in which we can believe with absolute confidence, it is the fact that Jesus Christ died, was buried, then conquered death and is now alive!

Creation and Resurrection

The universal reign of death in the world is explainable only in terms of the Creator's curse on man and his dominion because of his sin (Gen. 3:17-19). Since God the Creator was the One who imposed this universal law of death, it is only He who can supersede and change it.

The unique bodily resurrection of Jesus Christ is clear proof that He is God, as well as man, because only God could conquer death. The great Creator became the Son of Man, that He might die for man's sin, but He also remained God and death could not hold Him!

His first great work --Creation--was finished from the foundation of the world (Gen. 2:1-3; Heb. 11:3). Creation was perfect and complete from the beginning; it needed no further assistance from an imaginary process of evolution to finish the job.

In the same way, His second work-- Redemption--was now also perfect and complete. After suffering hell, itself--spiritual death--on the cross, dying alone under all the weight of the sins of every man, He shouted in victory "It is finished!" (John 19:30). He dismissed His spirit from His body, allowing it to be buried in certain testimony that His death was also a physical death.

When He returned to the body three days later, imparting to it a glorious, eternal, resurrection life. He demonstrated to all men of all the ages that He indeed was the Creator, that the problem of sin had been solved, and that death had forever lost its sting.

The redemption price has been paid, and one day, "the [creation] itself also shall be delivered from the bondage of corruption into the glorious liberty of the children of God" (Ro. 8:21).

Until that day, when He "[makes] all things new" (Rev. 21:5), His promise of forgiveness, salvation, resurrection, and eternal life is available on an individual basis to every person who believes Him and accepts His Word. "For if, when we were enemies, we were reconciled to God by the death of his Son, much more, being reconciled, we shall be saved by his life" (Ro. 5:10).

∽ *10* ∽

What happened in The Throne Room of God?

The Blood Applied in Heaven

In the last chapter, we explored the series of events surrounding the resurrection of Jesus. As we left the grave site, Jesus was yet to complete His assignment. The full atonement for the sins of all mankind. If you recall Jesus said to Mary "Do not touch me, for I have yet not ascended to the Father".

In the following passage, we see that Jesus is about to enter the heavenly throne room of God, the Father. The passage then goes on to state the Jesus enters the throne room with His own blood. The bible gives no information on how Jesus accumulated His blood. However, the scripture emphatically states that Jesus (Our High Priest) takes His sacrificial blood to be placed on the mercy seat.

Hebrews 9:11-13 (KJV)
11 But Christ being come a high priest of good things to come, by a greater and more perfect tabernacle, not made with hands, that is to say, not of this building;
12 Neither by the blood of goats and calves, but by His own blood he entered in once into the holy place, having obtained eternal redemption for us.
13 For if the blood of bulls and of goats, and the ashes of a heifer sprinkling the unclean, sanctified to the purifying of the flesh:

The Approach to The Throne

The Lord tells us that everything is a type and shadow of those things that are eternal.

We see a perfect picture on Christ' approach to the throne in the story of Queen Esther. Esther acted as an intercessor for the children of Israel that were in captivity. Haman wanted to kill all the Jews. That is when Mordechai, Esther's uncle, told her that she was born for such a time as this.

However, to intercede on behalf of her people, Esther would have to go into the Kings throne room to plead her case unannounced. According to the Medes-Persians this was strictly prohibited. If Esther were to approach the throne room unannounced she risked being put to death. The only exception to this was if the king were to extend his scepter.

So, with the Jewish people fasting in prayer, Esther goes to the kings' throne room. Upon arrival, a deafening silence envelopes the throne room. The question on the minds of those in the room was. Will the king extend his scepter or would Esther be put to death? As soon as the king recognizes his beautiful wife; he king extends his scepter showing favor and acceptance.

Now let us move to the heavenly throne room of The Almighty, Holy, Holy, Holy God. I can just see the throne room.

On the throne is God Himself with the Holy Spirit.

Directly in front of Him Is the Ark of the Covenant with the Mercy Seat on the top.

Around the throne are the four and twenty elders, Cherubim, Seraphim

On one side you have, Zoe Spirits, Archangels, Messenger angels, Warring Angel, Ministering Spirits etc.

On the other side you have Adam, Abraham, Isaac, Jacob, Moses, Joshua, Miriam, Deborah, Rahab, Ruth, Boaz and all the saints that been released from Paradise at the resurrection of Jesus.

As was the case with Esther, so similarly we see Jesus approach to the throne.

As Jesus approaches the entrance to throne, in His hand is His own blood to be offered on the Mercy Seat that is before God.

With all in attendance, A Holy Hush overshadows the throne room of God. The silence is deafening, you could hear a pin drop. All eyes were on God. You see this was the first time that the Father has looked upon His beloved son, the very son that He had to turn His back on. And then the Father extends the golden scepter to His beloved son. Jesus slowly begins His trip the Ark of the Covenant carrying His own blood. The question on the mind of those witnessing this event was is this what we have been waiting for all these years? Will this act finally deal with the sin issue once and for all times? When Jesus arrives at the Ark of the Covenant, He pours His own blood upon the Mercy seat. When he has completed this the Glory of God Consumes the Blood offering declaring it acceptable. The Shekinah Glory radiates instantly and celebration begins like never before. This was to declare that the atoning work of Jesus Christ was now completely satisfied.

Yet there was one other thing that the Lord revealed to me.

We all know that Sin (originated) was found in Lucifer while he was in heaven. When Lucifer was expelled the heavenly temple was never sanctified. The only thing that sanctifies is the blood. If you recall when Moses was to dedicate the tabernacle, God instructed Moses to anoint all the furnishing in the tabernacle, including the golden candlestick, The table of shewbread, The altar of incense, The Ark of the Covenant. All were to be anointed with the blood.

So, Jesus, to complete His assignment anoints the Heavenly Holy of holies and the throne room of God the Father.

Paul tell us: "For Christ is not entered into the holy places made with hands, which are the figures of the true; but into heaven itself, now **TO APPEAR IN THE PRESENCE OF GOD FOR US"** (Hebrews 9:24). Jesus had to appear before God the Father with the shed blood. This is why He told Mary not to touch Him when He arose from the dead. "Jesus saith unto her, TOUCH ME **NOT; FOR I AM NOT YET ASCENDED TO MY FATHER**: but go to my brethren, and say unto them, I ascend unto my Father, and your Father; and to my God, and your God" (John 20:17).

If Mary had touched Jesus, the blood sacrifice would have been tainted with corruption. Jesus was heading toward heaven with the blood which needed to be applied to the mercy seat in Heaven. "Now of the things which we have spoken this is the sum: We have such an **HIGH PRIEST**, who is set on the right hand of the throne of the Majesty in the heavens" (Hebrews 8:1). Jesus is our High Priest! "Seeing then that we have a great **HIGH PRIEST**, that is passed into the heavens, **JESUS THE SON OF GOD...**" (Hebrews 4:14). Jesus' tabernacle is in Heaven, not on earth, "A minister of the sanctuary, and of the true tabernacle, which the Lord pitched, and not man" (Hebrews 8:2).

The Heavenly Mercy Seat

The Mercy seat is located within this tabernacle in Heaven, just as it was in the Old Testament tabernacle. God required for the Jewish High Priest to perform a ceremonial sacrifice once per year to atone for the sins of the Israelite people. The sacrifice pictured the coming Messiah who would someday die on the cross for the sins of all people. This ceremonial event ceased when Christ died on the cross because the shadow of things to come was now obsolete, Jesus fulfilled the prophecy.

The Old Testament tabernacle, priests, Holy of Holies and mercy seat were all a shadow (or replica) of the Tabernacle and in Heaven. "Who serve unto the **EXAMPLE AND SHADOW OF HEAVENLY THINGS**, as Moses was admonished of God when he was about to make the tabernacle: for, See, saith he, that thou make all things according to the pattern shewed to thee in the mount" (Hebrews 5:8).

The Old Testament tabernacle was a mirror image of the tabernacle in Heaven where Christ would someday make the ultimate sacrifice with His shed blood. Jesus used His own blood to pay for our sins. Christ's blood was applied to the Mercy Seat in Heaven. For anyone to teach that Jesus' blood has no redeeming power is a false prophet. To diminish the necessity of Christ's blood sacrifice is an abomination unto God.

The Blood Applied in Heaven

Just as the Jewish high priest was required to enter into the Holy of Holies once a year, likewise Christ had to enter into the Holy of Holies to appear before God. The Old Testament tabernacle was divided into three parts: the outer court, the inner court and then the Holy of Holies. Only certain priests who followed certain cleansing rituals were allowed into the inner court. Absolutely no one could enter into the Holy of Holies except a certain high priest once a year. Disobeying certain rules meant death.

For example, if the high priest entered into the Holy of Holies without the lamb's blood, God would have killed him. The blood atonement was sacred to God. Christ's blood is a serious matter to God. We must not make light of something that God holds dear. "Forasmuch as ye know that ye were not redeemed with corruptible things, as silver and gold, from your vain conversation received by tradition from your fathers; But **WITH THE PRECIOUS BLOOD OF CHRIST**, as of a lamb without blemish and without spot" (1st Peter 1:18,19). Jesus is precious! Jesus' blood is precious!

Carefully note that the word "atonement" is an Old Testament word which means "to cover." Jesus DIDN'T merely cover our sins, He took them away forever with His blood. Amen! This is why, when speaking of Christ's work of redemption, I refer to His "blood sacrifice" instead of using the word "atonement."

107

What a wonderful and loving God, that He would provide salvation to us through His own suffering and sacrifice. Surely, there is no greater love than this. Do you fail to see God's love toward mankind? If so, it is only because of your sinful unbelief. Believe, my friend, and let God have His way with your heart.

The LITERAL Blood of Jesus Had to be Applied to the Mercy Seat in Heaven

The great Bible teacher, **M.R. DeHaan, M.D**. has it 100% correct when he states concerning the blood of Jesus...

The blood was to be sprinkled, remember, on the mercy seat right after the death of the substitutionary animal of sacrifice, Now Christ is, of course, our substitute. He was slain for us upon the cross, and entered into death for us, and when He arose, He immediately went to heaven, entered into the holy of holies in heaven, sprinkled His precious blood upon the mercy seat before the throne of God, and forever settled the sin questions, and delivered us from the curse of the law. This is clearly taught in the New testament. Hebrews 9:12 is very definite on this:

"But by His own blood he entered in once into the holy place, having obtained eternal redemption for us."

The Bible also makes plain when He accomplished this. On the morning of the resurrection He meets Mary at the tomb. As soon as Mary recognized Him, Jesus emphatically says to her: "Touch me not"; and then He proceeds immediately to give the reason why Mary is not permitted to touch Him at all.

"For I am not yet ascended to my Father: but go to my brethren, and say unto them, I ascend unto my Father, and your Father; and to my God, and your God." (John 20:17)

Literally the Lord Jesus Christ said, "Touch me not; for I now am about to ascend unto my Father." We can understand this action when we remember the high priest after he had offered the sacrifice, was to enter the Holy of Holies, before he did anything else, with the precious blood. No one was allowed to approach him. Everyone was shut out until this was completely done. In the record of the meeting with Mary we have the fulfillment of this type. Here Mary meets her great High Priest, just arisen from the tomb, but before He had entered the holy of holies with the reconciling blood. And so, He says to her, "TOUCH ME NOT."

SOURCE: *The Tabernacle*, by M.R. DeHaan, M.D., ISBN 0-310-23491-3, page 129.

Jesus' Blood Washes Our Sins Away

"Having therefore, brethren, boldness to enter into the holiest **BY THE BLOOD OF JESUS**, by a new and living way, which he hath consecrated for us, through the veil, that is to say, his flesh; And having an high priest over the house of God. Let us draw near with a true heart in full assurance of faith, <u>having our hearts sprinkled from an evil conscience</u>, and our bodies washed with pure water" (Heb. 10:19-22). As believers, we are not to live with guilt over the past. We are to sprinkle our past sins and mistakes with the blood of Jesus. What this means is that you must realize in your mind that Christ's blood has washed your sins away and they are gone forever. "...Unto him that loved us, and **WASHED US FROM OUR SINS IN HIS OWN BLOOD**" (Rev. 1:5).

Have your sins been forgiven? Jesus has made the provision for your forgiveness. All you have to do is say "yes" to He Who knocks at the door of your heart and invite Him in, "Behold, I **STAND AT THE DOOR, AND KNOCK**: if any man hears my voice, and open the door, I will come in to him, and will sup with him, and he with me" (Revelation 3:20). Is Jesus knocking at the door to your heart? Let Him in. By the way, you can't invite Him in twice. Would you invite someone into your house who has already entered? Of course not! The same is true with salvation—If saved, always saved. ONCE Jesus Christ comes in, He never leaves. You can't throw Him out either! You might stick Him in a closet and forget He's there, just like any other old stuff in the attic or closet, but He's still there. You absolutely CANNOT lose your salvation. Whether or not you have ever been saved is another story. Many folks who think they are saved are NOT! Only Jesus, trust in Him.

Christ Atoned ONCE For ALL

"Who needeth not daily, as those high priests, to offer up sacrifice, first for his own sins, and then for the people's: for this he did **ONCE**, when he offered up himself" (Hebrews 7:27). This is important to understand, Jesus died and atoned for our sins **ONCE**. Jesus is not still hanging on a cross as Catholicism portray Him. The Catholic religion teaches that when you take the Lord's Supper (Holy Eucharist) that the bread and juice literally become the blood and body of Jesus Christ when digested. They believe this is necessary for renewed spiritual life. This of course is as ridiculous as it is totally unscriptural. The bread and juice simply remind us of what Christ did for us to redeem us unto Himself, no more.

There is NO magic power in partaking of the Lord's Supper. Jesus does NOT die every time. Catholicism teaches that Jesus dies over and over again. This is NOT what the Bible teaches. Jesus died ONCE, He shed His blood ONCE, He applied the blood ONCE—it is finished. "So, Christ was **ONCE** offered to bear the sins of many" (Hebrews 9:28). "By the which will we are sanctified through the offering of the body of Jesus Christ **ONCE** for all" (Hebrews 10:10). Jesus did NOT stay on the cross bless God, He did NOT remain in the grave, He arose triumphant over death and is alive forever more. Thanks, be to His name.

~ *11* ~

The Power of the Blood

1 Pet 1.18-23

[**The Incredible Power of Jesus' Blood.** – The Bible has much to say about the incredible, precious blood of our Lord Jesus Christ. Let us never forget how the Word of God and our Christian lives are touched by the blood of our loving Lord and Savior, Jesus Christ.]

[**Jesus' Unique Blood** - Let us recall that the blood of our savior is not like our blood. Our blood poured into our veins from our father's, who received it from their fathers, who, in the heritage of things received their blood from Adam. Hence, Adam's sinful blood pulses through our veins by inheritance. In this sense, we are born sinners.]

[But our Lord, Jesus Christ, did not have Adam as His father. Instead through the undeniable virgin birth; Jesus had His Father's blood pulsing through His veins. Jesus' blood was, and is, God's blood. Hence, Jesus' blood is absolutely unique and Jesus truly is *".. . the only begotten of the father. .."* (John 1.4; 3.16; 1 John 4.9). Jesus' blood was not like our blood, and therefore offers what only the blood of God can offer us.]

[Lose sight of the uniqueness of Jesus' blood and you will lose sight of much of the Gospel and the essence of the salvation offered to us by God. There is absolutely nothing in this world that compares to the salvation offered us through the gospel of the Lord, Jesus Christ. There is absolutely nothing in this world that can compare to the precious blood of the Lord, Jesus Christ.]

Jesus' Blood Has,

1. **Redeeming Power (1 Cor 6.19-20; 1 Pet 1.18-19; Titus 3.5)**
[- To redeem something is to buy something. The Bible says,]

1 Corinthians 6:19-20
19 What? know ye not that your body is the temple of the Holy Ghost which is in you, which ye have of God, and ye are not your own?
*20 **For ye are bought with a price**: therefore, glorify God in your body, and in your spirit, which are God's.*

[This tells us that as Christians we were bought by God. He paid a price for us and as a result we belong to Him and we ought to live our lives as though we are His. Now, **How much were you worth?**]

1 Peter 1:18-19
18 Forasmuch as ye know that ye were not redeemed with corruptible things, as silver and gold, from your vain conversation received by tradition from your fathers;
*19 **But with the precious blood of Christ, as of a lamb without blemish and without spot:***

[It cost God the very best that heaven had to offer to redeem you. It cost God the life and blood of the Lord Jesus Christ. It cost God His only begotten Son. What an incredible price your Heavenly Father was willing to pay for you.]

[**No silver or Gold** – Notice that nothing in this world could have purchased your redemption. Silver and gold are purchased through the sweat of your brow. Hence, the silver and gold here represent your good works. The Bible says,

[*Titus 3:5 Not by works of righteousness which we have done, but according to his mercy he saved us, by the washing of regeneration, and renewing of the Holy Ghost;*]

[There is nothing you could ever do to secure your own redemption or salvation, but you can be redeemed by the blood of the Lord, Jesus Christ.]

2. **Atoning Power (Heb. 9.22)** [– Atoning Efficacy – Atone means to make compensation for or to pay the required price. Efficacy means the power to produce effects. Hence, Jesus' blood alone has the power to purchase your redemption. Nothing else can take away your sins and their penalties. Blood has always been required for the remission of sins. The Bible says,]

[Hebrews 9:22 *And almost all things are by the law purged with blood;* ***and without shedding of blood is no remission.]***

[Hence, the Old Testament sacrifices were required. But these sacrifices were mortal and corruptible. The Bible says,]

Hebrews 10:4 *For it is not possible that the blood of bulls and of goats should take away sins.*

Hebrews 10:11-12.
11 And every priest standeth daily ministering and offering oftentimes the same sacrifices, which can never take away sins:
12 But this man, after he had offered one sacrifice for sins forever, sat down on the right hand of God;

[Hence, the Old Testament sacrifices pointed to the one eternal sacrifice whose blood contained the atoning power to fully satisfy the required cost for our sins. This sacrifice was the Lord Jesus Christ, with His unique and perfect blood.]

[Only Jesus' blood has the atoning power needed to take way your sins and their terrible cost.]

3. Cleansing Power (1 John 1.7; Isa 1.18)

[**1 John 1:7** *But if we walk in the light, as he is in the light, we have fellowship one with another, **and the blood of Jesus Christ his Son cleanseth us from all sin.***]

[Mortal, corruptible blood has the power to stain and defile. Shed a bit of blood and you had better keep is from touching any garment that you value for its will cause a resilient stain. But the precious blood of our Lord, Jesus Christ is unique indeed for it has the power cleanse, not stain.]

[Isaiah, in referring to the cleansing blood of our Lord, Jesus Christ wrote,

[***Isaiah 1:18*** *Come now, and let us reason together, saith the Lord: though your sins be as scarlet, they shall be as white as snow; though they be red like crimson, they shall be as wool.*]

[Not only does the blood of Jesus cleanse but its purification, when applied is total and complete. Jesus' blood cleanses from ".. . all sin." There is no sin stain too resolute for the cleansing power of Jesus divine blood.]

4. Preserving Power (Exodus 12.13) [– In the Passover we see the Blood of the lamb, which was the foreshadow of the precious eternal blood of the Lamb of God, our Lord, Jesus Christ. The children of Israel were commanded to take a lamb and kill it. Tthen take its' blood and strike the door posts and the lintel of their door and to enter that house and eat that Passover lamb. During the night, as the death angel passed through the land of Egypt, he would take the first born of every house. But God said,]

Exodus 12:13 *And the blood shall be to you for a token upon the houses where ye are: **and when I see the blood**, I will pass over you, and the plague shall not be upon you to destroy you, when I smite the land of Egypt.*

[It was the blood of that lamb that provided the preserving power for those who applied the blood and trusted in its' promise. Our text declares,]

1 Peter 1:18-19
18 Forasmuch as ye know that ye were not redeemed with corruptible things, as silver and gold, from your vain conversation received by tradition from your fathers;
*19 But with the precious blood of Christ, **as of a lamb without blemish and without spot:***

[Notice this phrase and how it undeniably speaks of the Passover lamb and its' preserving blood. The precious blood of the Lord, Jesus Christ has preserving power.]

5. **Pleading Power (Heb. 12.24; Gen 4.10; Num. 35.33; Luke 23.34)** [– C.H. Spurgeon called this Pleading Prevalence.]

   *Hebrews 12:24 And to Jesus the mediator of the new covenant, **and to the blood of sprinkling, that speaketh better things than that of Abel.***

[Did you know that your blood has a voice? It cries out to God, and God hears its' plea. Spurgeon noted that Abel's blood plead with God for vengeance.]

Genesis 4:10 And he said, What hast thou done? the voice of thy brother's blood crieth unto me from the ground.

[Be careful that you do not underestimate the pleading power of one's blood. The cry from shed blood is loud and persuasive in the ears of almighty God. The shedding of blood is a serious matter with God. The Bible says,]

Numbers 35:33 So ye shall not pollute the land wherein ye are: for blood, it defileth the land: and the land cannot be cleansed of the blood that is shed therein, but by the blood of him that shed it.

[Imagine how loud the cries must be from the blood of millions of innocent unborn babies murdered for convenience and commerce in America and our world through abortion. Imagine the deafening cries from all the bloodshed in our sinful world these days. What an incredible cry this must be.]

[Then there is Jesus' precious blood and its' cry before His Father. Again, our text reads,]

***Hebrews 12:24** And to Jesus the mediator of the new covenant, and to the blood of sprinkling, that speaketh better things than that of Abel.*

[What is the plea of Jesus precious blood? What is the cry of the blood of God's only begotten Son? The blood of Jesus cries out,]

Luke 23:34. .. Father, forgive them; for they know not what they do. .

[Glory to God, Our Lord and Savior's blood calls out for your forgiveness and total cleansing.]

6. **Consecrating Power (Heb 9.14)** [– The precious shed blood of the Lord Jesus Christ, when properly seen in it sacrifice and compassion has the ability to bring a rebellious, sinful heart and mind into submissive, sacrificial obedience to the Heavenly Father. The Bible reads,]

Hebrews 9:14 How much more shall the blood of Christ, who through the eternal Spirit offered himself without spot to God, purge your conscience from dead works to serve the living God?

[The blood of our Lord, Jesus Christ has the power to transform your mind and the way you think.]

7. <u>Positioning</u> Power (Heb. 10.19-20)

Hebrews 10:19-20
19 Having therefore, brethren, boldness to enter into the holiest by the blood of Jesus,
20 By a new and living way, which he hath consecrated for us, through the veil, that is to say, his flesh:

[Through the precious blood of our Lord, Jesus Christ we have been granted the position of children of the King. Jesus when He ascended on high sat down at the right hand of the Father (Acts 2.33; 7.35). Now we as joint heirs with Christ (Rom 8.17) have come into the holy of holies and stand in the very presence of our Heavenly Father. A position of great stature, authority, power and security.]

8. <u>Confirming</u> Power (Heb. 13.20)

Hebrews 13:20 Now the God of peace, that brought again from the dead our Lord Jesus, that great shepherd of the sheep, **through the blood of the everlasting covenant,**

[No covenant is confirmed by God without the shedding of blood., The New Testament speaks of Jesus' blood as the "blood of the everlasting covenant." Hence, confirming our eternal and everlasting security. Through Jesus' precious blood we can be secure in our eternal life because Jesus' blood is the confirming agent of our covenant with our Heavenly Father. Praise God for the confirming power of Jesus blood!]

9. Quickening Power (John 6.53; Lev. 17.11; Eph. 2.5-6) [– This is the power to instill life. The Bible reads,]

[John 6:53 Then Jesus said unto them, Verily, verily, I say unto you, except ye eat the flesh of the Son of man, **and drink his blood, ye have no life in you.]**

[It is the precious blood of the Lord Jesus Christ that pours the spiritual life of Christ into our hearts and souls.

Perhaps, this is what God was implying, at least in part, when He said,]

Leviticus 17:11 For the life of the flesh is in the blood: ..

[It is through the precious blood of our Lord Jesus Christ that we are brought into the abounding life that our Lord desired for us to know and have (John 10.10). Paul wrote,]

Ephesians 2:5-6
5 Even when we were dead in sins, hath quickened us together with Christ, (by grace ye are saved;)
6 And hath raised us up together, and made us sit together in heavenly places in Christ Jesus:

10. Overcoming Power (Rev. 12.10-11)

Rev. 12:10-11
10 And I heard a loud voice saying in heaven, now is come salvation, and strength, and the kingdom of our God, and the power of his Christ: for the accuser of our brethren is cast down, which accused them before our God day and night.
*11 **And they overcame him by the blood of the Lamb**, and by the word of their testimony; and they loved not their lives unto the death.*

[No matter how desperate your tribulation and trials may be. You can overcome them all through the strengthening power of the precious blood of our Lord, Jesus Christ. When you are in desperate time, remember and plead the blood. How will pleading the blood help you in those times? It will remind you of the comforting love and goodness of your Heavenly Father, and assure you of the victory that is on your horizon. It will help you recall that they may take this mortal life, but they cannot touch your promised and secure everlasting life with bountiful rewards.]

11. <u>Melting</u> Power (Zech. 12.10)

*[Zech. 12:10 And **I will pour upon** the house of David, and upon the inhabitants of Jerusalem, the spirit of grace and of supplications: **and they shall look upon me whom they have pierced, and they shall mourn for him, as one mourneth for his only son, and shall be in bitterness for him, as one that is in bitterness for his firstborn.**]*

[When they pierced our Lord what came out? Water and blood (John 19.34). The precious shed blood of our Lord, Jesus Christ speaks of the suffering, sacrificial love of God toward sinful, lost and rebellious people. This love of God, wrapped up in the Blood of Christ, has the power to melt the hardest heart.]

[Do not pound upon the hardened hearts of the wayward with the hammer of the gospel for you will just callus and harden those hearts; but pour upon them the love of God through the blood of Christ and melt those calluses' away. It is the precious blood of our Lord, Jesus Christ that can melt and change the hardest hearts.]

1 Peter 1:18-23

18 Forasmuch as ye know that ye were not redeemed with corruptible things, as silver and gold, from your vain conversation received by tradition from your fathers;

19 But with the precious blood of Christ, as of a lamb without blemish and without spot: 20 Who verily was foreordained before the foundation of the world, but was manifest in these last times for you,

21 Who by him do believe in God, that raised him up from the dead, and gave him glory; that your faith and hope might be in God.

22 Seeing ye have purified your souls in obeying the truth through the Spirit unto unfeigned love of the brethren, see that ye love one another with a pure heart fervently:

23 Being born again, not of corruptible seed, but of incorruptible, by the word of God, which liveth and abideth forever.

THE SALVATION PRAYER

Please note: The Salvation Prayer (sometimes referred to as the Sinner's Prayer) below, is not an "official prayer" but rather a sample prayer to follow when asking Jesus into your heart. You can pray to God in your own words if you choose.

Regarding the location of the Sinner's Prayer in the Bible, there isn't one mentioned. It is only implied. The basis of the Sinner's Prayer comes from Ro. 10:9-10. "That if thou shalt confess with thy mouth the Lord Jesus, and shalt believe in thine heart that God hath raised him from the dead, thou shalt be saved. For with the heart man believeth unto righteousness; and with the mouth confession is made unto salvation."

SALVATION PRAYER

Dear God in heaven, I come to you in the name of Jesus. I acknowledge to You that I am a sinner, and I am sorry for my sins and the life that I have lived.; I need your forgiveness.

I believe that your only begotten Son Jesus Christ shed His precious blood on the cross at Calvary and died for my sins, and I am now willing to turn from my sin.

You said in Your Holy Word, Romans 10:9 that if we confess the Lord our God and believe in our hearts that God raised Jesus from the dead, we shall be saved.

Right now, I confess Jesus as the Lord of my soul. With my heart, I believe that God raised Jesus from the dead. This very moment I accept Jesus Christ as my own personal Savior and according to His Word, right now I am saved.

Thank you, Jesus, for your unlimited grace which has saved me from my sins. I thank you Jesus that your grace never leads to license, but rather it always leads to repentance. Therefore, Lord Jesus transform my life so that I may bring glory and honor to you alone and not to myself.

Thank you, Jesus, for dying for me and giving me eternal life. AMEN

About the Authors

Apostle Halton "Skip" Horton

In 1984 God honored Apostle Horton with a vision to teach the whole bible without denominational persuasion with the zeal of God performing it, and The Bright Star Church was birthed as a ministry of faith. God's vision was that of a growing church with people coming from the North, South, East and West. Today, The Day Star Tabernacle International is alive and vibrant with God's Word.

The present location of the church 8200 Highway 166, Douglasville, GA was occupied in May 2000. The 17.63 acres of the campground includes: The Sanctuary, The Family Life Center, The Sonshine Gymnasium, The Courts of Praise Tennis Courts, The Agape Place, The Fun Zone and our new Home of the Saints Softball field and picnic area. There are currently 42 ministries in place for the edifying and building up of those inside and outside of the Body of Christ. The current sanctuary houses our Stars of Heaven Children's Nursery and The Christian Life School of Theology.

We are a body of people who believe we should carry God's Word and share it with others. The "Lion of Judah" television ministry is seen locally on AIB (Atlanta Interfaith Broadcast) and WATC.

The Lord has blessed us with a corporate anointing for traveling to minister to various churches nationally and internationally as God leads.

We have a ministry of an evangelistic thrust reaching communities, prisons and hospitals. We are a body of believers that are *excited and jubilant about worshipping and praising* God with an intense enthusiasm.

Apostle Horton is frequently asked to minister on prophecy and eschatology. God has placed an anointing on him to proclaim and teach about end-times from the book of Revelation and to equip us to *"see beyond what we see"*. With his teaching of prophecy, Apostle Horton is the author of several books, ***"God's Numbers and What They Mean", "Oh! How the Days Are Telling", "Redeemed Talk", "The Intersection of Praise and Thanksgiving Boulevard", "There's Power in Paying Attention", The Foundation of Salvation", "Kingdomize Your Thinking", and the new release "The Watchman Sees Book I" , "The Watchman Sees Book II" and "Release for Increase" ."*** *Apostle Horton has a prophetic calling in teaching other books of the Bible, allowing the Body of Christ to understand the Spirit of Wisdom and the revelation in the knowledge of* **Him** *(Jesus Christ).*

Notable Employment/Education: Assistant Vice President for ten years, United First Mortgage; Served in U. S. Army (data processing) with a top security clearance and The Department of Revenue.

Doctor of Philosophy in Counseling, Trinity Christian University; Master Degree of Sociology, Atlanta Univ., Bachelor of Arts Degree Sociology/Counseling, Fort Valley State College.

Additional ministries and community involvement include;

- Member of the Douglas County Faith Based Community Initiative

- Morris Cerullo World Evangelism Board of Elders

- Member of the International Coalition of Apostles

The Day Star Tabernacle International is in covenant with over 1,000 other ministries throughout the world including India, Philippines, Pakistan, London, Canada, Africa, Malaysia, Singapore and Mexico. Apostle Horton has dedicated this book to the five-fold ministry around the world with special acknowledgment to the 7000More International Covenant Church Fellowship.

*Praise **God** from whom all blessings flow. We give **God** all honor and praise for the things **He** has done.*

Apostle Frank Baio, PhD.

In October of 1987, the Lord spoke to my heart. He said, "Arise, my son, now is the time for which I have been preparing you I have called you to preach and teach My Word to My people. I, the Lord, will change the lives of those who hear and obey My Word. I will cause them to be victorious. I will bring about a healing in their hearts and lives and wherever they go. My son, my call has been upon you from childhood. Now, choose you this day whom you will serve." For I, the Lord your God, am with you. I will never leave you nor forsake you.

Frank Baio is an anointed and gifted man of God. He is sensitive to the Holy Spirit and flows with the Spirit. In every service, the Holy Spirit Manifests Himself powerfully. God confirms His Word with miracles, signs and wonders.

Frank and his wife, Fran, have been married since 1969.
Frank has pastored churches for 17 years.
Apostle Baio has been on the faculty of the Institute of Ministry in Bradenton, Florida since 1998 and is one of the most popular teachers.
Frank is an international evangelist, conducting services in the U.S.A. and overseas.

Many have been mentored by this man of God and are actively ministering around the world.
Apostle Baio recently received a PhD. in Sacred letters

Frank is Vice -President of Ministerial Affairs for Linkforce International, an International Ministry, reaching out to third world countries.

Apostle Baio is under the apostolic coverings of the following Apostles:
Apostle Skip Horton, Daystar International Ministerial Fellowship. Douglasville, Ga.
Apostle Rufus Troup, Solid Rock Apostolic Ministries, Cutler Ridge, Florida
Apostle Verbert C. Anderson, Jesus is Lord Worship Center, Miami, Florida

Apostle Baio has Co-Authored Two several books - The revelations series "The Watchman Sees Book I", "The Watchman Sees Book II-Seeing Beyond What You See". He has also authored "Allah Is Not Our God", "The Demise Of The Republic", "God's Word Is A Medicine", "You Can Be A Giant Killer, Too!", and "The Overview of the Old Testament".

These Books are designed to bring revelation knowledge to the body of Christ, especially as we approach the imminent return of Our Lord and Savior Jesus Christ.

In all your getting, get understanding. (Prov. 4:7)

Apostle Frank Baio, PhD.

921 Faith Circle East #70

Bradenton, Florida 34212

E-mail: fcap826@gmail.com

Cell Phone   # 941-779-8324

Home Phone # 941-746-5431

Made in the USA
Columbia, SC
02 October 2021

46185604R00075